DON'T FORGET TO LOCK IT AWAY!

First published in Great Britain in 2011 by Marsons
© Monika Sears 2010
Printed in Great Britain by Lightning Source

Typeset in Arno Pro
Text design by Rachel Jackson
Cover design by Edoardo Sears

The moral right of the author has been asserted.

All rights reserved. Without limiting the rights under copyright reserved above, no part of this publication may be reproduced, stored or introduced into a retrieval system, or transmitted, in any form or by any means (electronic, mechanical, photocopying, recording or otherwise), without the prior written permission of both the copyright owner and the publisher of this book.

A CIP catalogue record of this book is available from the British Library.
ISBN 978-0-9517220-5-3
www.marsonsbooks.com

DON'T FORGET TO LOCK IT AWAY!

by Monika Sears with Ruth Sands

Marsons London

OUR THANKS

To our parents, who managed to drag us out of the inferno and made new lives for themselves and above all, for us. Our thanks barely covers what we owe them.

To our ex-husbands, who rarely trod on our Glendale toes.

To Rosemary, staunch, reliable and who stood us in good stead.

To Judy, who helped us to launch it, who gently corrected mistakes of grammar, punctuation and sense. Her enthusiasm has kept ours stoked.

To Rachel who has made a good looking book out of a raw computer file.

To Eduardo who designed the cover.

To our colleagues and customers who kept us on our toes for so many years and who remain suspended, like flies in amber, in the Glendale Day Books.

DEDICATION

To our sons, Philippe, Paul, Ian, Marc and Oliver, who grew into interesting men, perhaps because of all the boxes of books in their young lives.

Before we begin …

Ruth and I …

We were introduced to each other by the headmistress of our sons' new school, who thought that we might get on. The little boys were to start nursery school the following term. Ruth had only recently moved into the district and did not know many people in the neighbourhood, so she gave her my telephone number.

One of us was born in the middle of trampled Europe, one was born at its eastern reaches. One had been smuggled to the West, the other escaped a little later. We spoke one language to our parents, another to our children. Our rootlessness was solid. We got on.

Ruth had not lived in England for more than three or four years. She did not have the comfort of family and old familiar friends around her, so she used to pack her small son into her minute car and go off on expeditions. She discovered parks with swings and shops selling the slightly weird and wonderful. She came back from one such expedition with five old children's books, fairly tatty or just perhaps well-loved. Knots of fairies drawn by Arthur Rackham. A Dulac princess desolate atop twenty mattresses with a single pea between her and a good night's rest. A small book in the shape of a rugby ball, with boys playing the game from page to bright page, undisturbed by mud. Who was Ernest Nister? Who was Henty with all that derring-do between sturdy cloth covers? All names familiar to children who had not dropped into England past their early childhood, but new to us.

I had read English at university, ploughed my way through the textual intricacies of Hamlet, met Grendel's mother head-on, weighed the merits of Pope and Dryden and even glanced fleetingly at the literature of Europe yet never had even the most lowly lecturer mentioned books written for children. In my time I had passed rapidly from Enid Blyton (easy) to Alice in Wonderland who had made me sick with all her claustrophobic rabbit holes and changes of size, to Dickens (difficult). It had never occurred to me that in my distant childhood, I had thus progressed from children's books to the grown-up kind, worthy of attention and ultimately seminars and Lit. Crit.

Ruth and I had been friends for some five years, our young sons were going together to their school round the corner, we shared shopping, rowdy week-ends and the ups and downs of our daily lives. With those first five books, we had plunged into the world of childhood, its history, the concept of childhood as a condition worthy of notice rather than just a messy stage to be survived with as little nuisance to the adult world as possible. When did children first have books written for their delight and not just for the nurture of their pagan little souls? When did the first spoonful of sugar appear to sweeten the tedium of learning the rivers of Europe and the kings of England by rote?

We bought a few more books. Then we found some in much better condition, so we sold most of the first batch. Within two years, we had become booksellers in a very modest way. Then we rented a small corner in an antique market in London and from there we graduated to a Book Room in an Antique Gallery (the difference was the carpet and the rent). By this time our interest had broadened to include the people who impinged on children's lives, teachers, tutors, governesses; parents kept fairly clear of the whole business. The shelves of illustrated books grew. Ruth became interested in modern first editions. I loved the books produced to ease the way of the nouveaux riches into the ways of civilised society and after the First World War, to help the nouveaux poor, suddenly bereft of maid, cook and butler, to keep their end up.

Somehow, without ambition or intent, we became booksellers.

We bought books at auction, from fellow booksellers who had acquired books outside their specialised fields but central to ours. We bought books offered by our customers, sometimes unwanted books, libraries left by aunts where only the carved mahogany bookcase was of interest to the nephews. We sold to anyone who wanted to buy a book. Well, almost anyone.

When our first tentative steps into the world of bookselling had become a little more assured and before we ventured into the wide world and rented a corner in the antique market, we decided that we needed a name. "Monika and Ruth" or even "Ruth and Monika" sounded like a dress agency or home caterers. Our surnames, in whatever order, were more knockabout than antiquarian booksellers, like "Box and Cox" or stand-up comics auditioning for ITV. We wanted something genderless, easy to pronounce and friendly. Roget yielded nothing that could be combined with the word "book" that had not already been nabbed. She lived in Glenilla Road and I lived in Daleham Gardens and when we tried various combinations of the two addresses, "Glendale" seemed to have more gravitas than "Daleilla". So we wrote our "M. & R. Glendale" in several hands, capitals and cursive, typed it, looked at it in the morning light and as the sun went down and decided that it would do nicely.

As we worked together over many years, we found our talents were complementary and that we propped up each other's weaknesses with little effort. Ruth repaired bindings, went to evening classes to learn how to rebind from scratch. She solved the mechanics of faulty and damaged moveable books which to me looked like cryptic crosswords where the clues were not even numbered. I restructured and painted all the missing heads and arms she needed to rebuild the pages. On our book-hunting expeditions, I did most of the driving and she navigated; I still have to turn the map upside down when going south. When we eventually started to take part in book fairs, first in England and then in America and Holland, Ruth could put the stand together and decorate it in the time it took me to unpack a single box and stare blankly at the contents laid out on the floor. But I was the best scavenger ever. Whatever we needed, I could find it or invent it, anything from an outsize book stand to a blackboard; she went through the auction catalogues. I did the accounts. She put together the orders. I packed them. Almost from the very beginning, we kept a day book. Like a ship's log, it summed up our position and the day's events. There was a reminder to buy a batch of lightbulbs, a howl of dismay at a book carelessly collated, pointed comments about the third visit that week from a gentleman who did not wash. We have a stack of twenty-five day books, a rare mixture of the erudite and the malicious, the personal and the administrative. There are questions about the first issue of Jane Eyre and her indecisive love life, uncensored invective in several languages about the cost of keeping the shop going. We have the day books to remind us of the quirky moments as booksellers, partners and above all, friends. And as we put our Glendale years in order, she is scouring the day books and I am doing the writing. So it's "Ruth and I ..."

Chapter 1

From book room to Antique Gallery

We found out that there existed a very good trade paper, The Bookdealer, which we studied together once a week so we had some idea who was interested in the same topics as we were. We typed our first slim catalogue with sweat and a lot of correcting fluid. Never having worked for an older, experienced bookseller where we would have gathered some basic skills, the mistakes we made, we made the hard way. "Mint condition" indicates that the book, complete with its dust jacket or presentation box, is in the condition in which it left the printers. The fact that it is not dog-eared and its cloth covers do not suffer from threadbare corners is not good enough; the fact that the contents are particularly interesting matters even less. "Mint condition" is an absolute. Our idea of mint condition, however, brought a lot of books scurrying back by return of post with some quite hurtful covering letters. "Very good condition" is a little more elastic. "Good" all on its own is damning with faint praise. We learnt that the number and position of leaping bunnies on the end papers of Beatrix Potter's little books was important in deciding whether the issue was a first or a third and even more importantly, that it mattered. We learnt about 4to and 8vo and 12mo and all the different shapes and sizes in between. We learnt that grown-ups dealing in children's books were not particularly interested in children or childhood. On the contrary, it was all those sticky little fingers over the decades that had reduced the pristine condition of a mint copy to one that was merely fair. The collectors, or on the other hand, the consumers at the end of the line of haggling and dealing, covered a whole range of motives and motivation, everything from the spaniel-eyed gentleman looking for the books nanny used to read to him to the academic librarian filling the gaps in the catalogue of the university collection with a hand-coloured alphabet.

After some eighteen months of reading and gathering and with two more catalogues behind us, where people had actually placed orders and kept the books we sent them, we decided it was time to display our precious hoard. There had been several phone calls asking for an appointment to see our stock. As we pushed our trolleys round Sainsbury's we talked about The Next Step. We had to have a Book Room.

Ruth lived in a three-storey town house where she had a small room at the top which would be perfect. We fitted it out with shelves, arranged the books to their best possible advantage, with the most beautifully illustrated or with the most decorative covers to the fore. We announced the good news in the trade paper and waited by the telephone. For a couple of days all was silence and then came the first call and then the second and the third. We jumped up and down like a couple of kids.

Most dealers in books, whether third generation professional or new amateurs, were men and tended to fit all too comfortably the story book image of the crusty old professor. Several made quite a performance of it, with half-lenses perched at the end of the nose, loose cardigan sagging over looser belly and that patina of shabbiness that tells the world that they are not in it for the money and have no intention of making any. There were, of course, a few who were younger and still frisky. The very few lady booksellers we met undoubtedly had beautiful souls and cultivated minds but it would be kinder to pass over the presentation of these virtues. There is no point in beating about the bush; we were both young, in our mid-twenties and where I can't comment objectively even today on my own plump little person, Ruth was extremely easy on the eye. She was tall, slim, with black hair and turquoise eyes and a very heavy French accent. For the average male Brit. A thick French accent in the mouth of a good-looking woman provokes a knee-jerk reaction and antiquarian books have nothing to do with it.

Looking back on it, for all our married status, we were both innocent and ignorant. We had both married young straight from the homes of protective mothers and doting fathers. Without even being aware of the advice of the inimitable Mrs Valentine, who had had much to say on the severe limitations of a proper young lady's education in the mid-1860s, we had followed it unwittingly in the mid-1960s. Neither of us had read much that would not have been approved by our dear Mamas or our former professors and the raunchiest film we had ever seen was probably Casablanca. So when Ruth, smiling sweetly, invited our gentleman caller to come with me upstairs, would you like to? Please? Do follow me, rolling her rrr's like barley sugar at the back of her little Parisian throat, she had no idea that the gentleman might be panting after her for anything but the sight of our Book Room. She had a surprise or two. We did not bother to wait for the third. The Book Room was transferred to a corner of the dining room in my house. Ground Floor. Street Level.

After a couple of years, I admit I was tired of the Book Room in my dining room. Our catalogues were doing so well. The telephone rang regularly and expectant faces now showed up at the door without warning, on the off chance ...

It was time to move to "premises" of our own. We were ready to launch Glendale upon the world. So we chose a very small stand in a slightly shabby antique market in the West End. Not so much a launch as a nervous toe in the water.

Our small unglamorous stand at Barrett Street Market was, for us, the big, tentative step into the world of bookselling. We were on public display. A small, passing public to be sure, sometimes shabby, at first not often interested in what we had to offer, but a public nonetheless.

"You mean people actually buy these?" asked one amazed woman, browsing from stand to stand in the hope of finding porcelain of some obscure manufacture.

"If you buy old books," some sniffed contemptuously, "they should, at the very least, be uniformly bound in glowing leather decorated with gilt bands and scrolls."

We had no answer, witty or otherwise, to offer but lowered our heads, apologetic for our lack of gold bands. We confided our pain and irritation to the Day Book. It took a long time to acquire that smirk of superior knowledge that tells the uninitiated that tooled leather, raised bands and fancy binding is but fodder for the uninitiated. The trouble was our tendency to giggle whenever that smug little smile appeared; Ruth had to avoid catching my eye. I had to turn my back. We never quite buckled our superiority into place securely.

The serious collector, the international dealer who sat in his assigned place at Christie's and was offered coffee in the hallowed precincts of Bloomsbury and Mayfair, did not visit Barrett Street. We were to make contact with this aristocratic layer of our business when we started visiting book fairs, then when we started exhibiting, as the quality of our stock, our knowledge and our confidence grew. It took time. In these early days of our bookselling lives, we had little enough of the rare and costly on our shelves to attract them. We relied, perhaps too seriously, on the subject matter, the illustrations, the history of our books. In the cloistered corner of my dining room, we had only been contacted by dealers and collectors, often only a little more senior and experienced than we were, curious to inspect the beginners. Nobody who wanted an original birthday present or a hilarious wedding gift for the couple who already had all the cutlery and crockery they could wish for had come to our door in our dining room days. During the early months in Barrett Street we learnt to look at our books as birthday presents and intellectual jokes (An illustrated copy of Paradise Lost to be presented to the bridegroom at his stag night party. Ha!). We learnt that there are bores with nothing to do but waste your time, and that empty chair on our stand, intended for the potential customer's comfort, was an open invitation to park a bum and start boring.

Some smiled, some were not pleased that we were no longer their private source. Now, new customers became regulars. We fired one or two people with our enthusiasm, people who had never thought to collect books or imagined that they could be accessible to those of slender means. We learnt to pile the spare chair with books and only put them to one side for those interested in books and not those determined to rest their aching feet and pour out their aching hearts.

It was during these early days in Barrett Street Market that our interest in children's books extended to the books that influenced children's lives, their school books, the miserable lives of their governesses and tutors on the outer edges of gentry, fallen upon hard times, used, abused, trying to keep their dignity sharing nursery tea, the stratum just above the servants' hall but unworthy of the family dining room. The Brontës, whether in first edition or paperback, spoke loudly of their plight. The books we looked at were the ones that helped the mistress of the house keep the governess in her place, what skills should be required of her, how much sugar should be her ration, her dress and comportment. Rarely was there any mention of the duty of the employer. Rarely was there any mention of the obedience and courtesy required of her pupils. Never a word about kindness. The tutor fared no better. Branwell's fall from grace was not unique.

We began to look at books, both in English and French, directed at the behaviour of women, whether married or to be married, all potential mothers. What she should be allowed to think, to read, what she should wear as matron and, almost inevitably, as widow. Her duty to her husband, unquestioning compliance in all matters; this was as near to the bedroom door as the books dared to creep. There were detailed chapters on the economic running of the household, the education of children, the hiring and firing of governesses and tutors, almost always written by reverend gentlemen, often celibate, unquestioning in their edicts, devoid of the least grain of humour. These neat handbooks, rigid morality in rigid bindings, were for the benefit of the lady, established or aspiring. The working class woman did not need to bother her head with such matters.

We looked at our children's books in a new light. There had been early, unsophisticated little books illustrated with crude woodcuts but as the wealthy nineteenth century progressed, children's books became objects of luxury to be kept away from jammy fingers and not to be flung across a bleak nursery in a temper tantrum. The illustrations were coloured by hand, then took advantage of the advances in colour printing, less time-consuming but not cheap. There were magnificent alphabets, books cut in the shape of footballs (rugby, of course), dolls and houses. There were books bound in pale cream cloth, kept pristine in pale cream boxes. And there were far too many that survived in excellent condition, to the delight of the twentieth-century collector, but how much to the delight of the original little owners?

So we sat in our Barrett Street corner, read, pondered, compared the different methods of colour printing, learnt the importance of collating accurately, of careful repairs and restoration. Family and friends, meanwhile, slowly accepted that we were serious. When two young women, married with children, go into partnership and start a business, their family and friends hold their breath.

"They don't know what they are letting themselves in for."

"They don't know the first thing about books (or flower arranging or catering or ...)."

"They'll row and that will be the end of that."

Every caveat was true. We did not know what we were letting ourselves in for, but we found out. If one of us made a boob, major or minor, we knew instinctively that piling on the blame would not solve anything so the blameless one rushed in to help. We discovered that we both had skills and talents we had never suspected and weaknesses that would better have been left undiscovered. We knew to fill in each other's gaps and to keep irritation down to a minimum. We did not know the first thing about books as a commodity but we both came from homes with books; reading was part of our daily lives. The world of dealing in books, of collecting, of rarity and curiosity, of university and municipal libraries were extensions of that basic interest. We would learn and would continue to learn until the day that Glendale folded its tent.

We rowed but it was never the end of that. After working together for so many years, we realised that family and friends had been breathing freely for quite a long time.

We had defied the laws of the fragility of partnerships, women's partnerships in particular and when we decided to close the shop, we disappointed them.

Chapter 2

Barrett Street Antique Market

An antique market had been an obvious step out of the closeted world of our book room. It offered us a comparatively inexpensive venue, surrounded by other dealers, possibly some passing trade and most importantly, a sense of security. There were several antique markets in London for us to look at, ranging from the elegant to the decidedly scruffy. We had chosen Barrett Street because of its position, just behind Oxford Street and thus very central, because it veered towards the scruffy end of the spectrum and it was one of the few where we could afford the rent. We had thrashed out the pros and cons in the check-out queue at the supermarket and in our respective kitchens surrounded by very small, very noisy boys.

Our husbands were supportive in a negative sort of way. They conceded that £200 each was not an outrageous amount to sink into the business, where sink was obviously going to be the operative word. Ruth's husband was prepared to listen to our plans and projects if we didn't go on about it for more than five minutes at a time. Mine, his own superior little smile in place, took the view that if wifey was happy with bookeys, than wifey should be indulged with bookeys. There was nothing useful to be had out of either of them. To do them justice, they were in the serious business of earning a living. Married at 18 and 21 respectively, Ruth and I had not done anything in the world of business or letters to engage consideration. We had produced four sons and a few good dinners, more the stuff of wifey than projected business plan. So we went ahead.

Once we were organised and ready to raise the blind on our new Book Room, more of a perch than a room, a narrow platform balanced over a staircase, we looked at our neighbours, each with his own small stand selling china, jewellery, corkscrews and bottle openers, lace and Victorian underwear. Our immediate neighbour was Peter, who sold antique jewellery of exceptional interest and quality. He told us so within a day or two of our arrival. The fact that he chose to do so from a small stand in an antique market rather than a prime position in the heart of Knightsbridge was a matter of personal choice made as a result of circumstances we could not begin to imagine. He flickered a smile as if about to reveal a secret drama but he only offered another cup of coffee. He was small, gentle, helpful. He came to work by car, in those days when it was still possible to park in central London, and since he lived just a little further north than we did, he didn't mind driving out of his way to pick us up. He said he enjoyed the company when we tried to thank him.

There were a great many quiet days at the market when nobody came and that was when we stallholders got to know each other. We learned a little about each other's wares and about each other's lives; why this one had chosen china and that one keys and locks.

"We're not actually married, Joe and I. We just live together," confessed Mary, guardian of the Locks and Keys stand. In the mid-1970s that was still indeed a confession. She was young enough to be his daughter, a top-heavy lump of a girl with mousy wisps of fringe falling into her eyes. He turned up seldom, snapped an order or two, sneered at her attempts to make some sort of a display of their thin stock and treated her like a mentally wanting pup. Then he hurried off to see to more important matters. It seemed unkind to tell her that it had never occurred to either of us that she and Joe might be anything other than employer and minion.

Robert and David were a couple and sold anything and everything as long as it was pretty. David was divinely handsome and did auditions. Robert looked after the stall and complained. He complained about the weather, the Labour Party, the rent, the ridiculous price of a decent haircut, dowdy swimsuits that did absolutely nothing for you, and David. David who did not pull his weight, sponged off him, didn't pay his share of the rent, and left his dirty water in the bath without giving himself the trouble of pulling the plug, would you believe? And then David would come in, arms flapping with excitement.

"A recall!!" They were down to three and he knew for a fact that the other two couldn't act for toffee apples and were real dawgs, so there was every chance he would get the part and then they would both be in clover. He went over every minute and second of the audition. He twirled and laughed and mimicked and Robert watched and glowed with generous pleasure, bathwater forgiven and forgotten.

Peter sat in our corner with one of our books on his lap and smiled at them with deep but distant understanding.

Then, one day he came to fetch me and I wasn't quite ready and so he came in and started talking to the husband and the sons. From there it was a short hop to inviting him and his wife to come and have dinner with us and of course, Ruth and her husband came as well. After that, the conversations on the way to work became slightly more intimate. After all, he now knew the families. The shrapnel from an ongoing matrimonial row was allowed to ricochet round his car instead of being contained in tight-lipped silence until the temper had cooled. We both found him so easy to talk to, his questions probing, his advice avuncular, full of good sense and humour. It was a pleasure to do what he suggested and bathe in his approval like good, sensible girls. He knew so much. He could place a quotation and identify the symphony playing on the car radio. He had met so many interesting people in that mysterious previous life of his. He dropped names, certainly, but without that tell-tale pause or flicker of the eye that makes sure that the name has been duly caught. This was his life as he had once lived it and this was his contribution to the friendship growing between the three of us.

"The first time I met Georg Solti he wasn't wearing socks."

And he tittered at the memory of a sockless Georg.

"Eric had such peculiar handwriting," he nodded over the steering wheel, "at least, I found it difficult enough to read."

Eric? Ah, yes, Big Brother must have been watching him; one had to let him know that the identity of the Eric with the bad handwriting had been recognised and the bad handwriting forgiven, in view of what he had written with it outside his illegible correspondence with Peter.

He took a very special interest in all our health problems. Ruth had suffered severe injuries in a car accident and he followed the progress of her rehabilitation, talked about the importance of exercise in its long-term maintenance, the name of every bone, muscle and nerve tripping off his tongue with the easy familiarity of one who has Gray's Anatomy at his finger tips.

"Appendicitis," he said quietly after I had tried to calm a bellowing No. 2 son on the telephone. "Take a taxi home and call an ambulance."

The appendix came out that afternoon.

His story came about a sliver at a time. Ruth would get the first paragraph and a week or two later I would get the fourth. Then he would go back to another part of his story but if we probed or tried to make sense of it, he would casually drift off to some other subject, the Test match or the government reshuffle. He had been a doctor. He was a doctor. He had not been struck off, anything but, only good sense had prevailed and he had retired from practice to prevent another tragedy. He was a surgeon and in that branch of the profession, tragedy is only a minute slip of the scalpel away. It had happened to him. He had not been blamed although there had been a nerve-racking investigation. He had been exonerated by his hospital and by his college but he felt that he could not and should not continue. He had retired immediately. Was there a slight tremor in his hands? He held out both hands over the steering wheel and peered at them accusingly. The income and the lifestyle had come down several notches, he admitted wryly, but gemmology had always been a hobby and it had proved a standby. He had qualified, of course. Barrett Street was the modest outlet he had chosen because it would be inappropriate and embarrassing to swan about in an upmarket setting and bump into former patients and colleagues. He was comfortable with the decision he had taken and so was his wife.

These snippets of information were never mentioned when his wife or our husbands were present, enjoying lunch or a cup of tea together. When I congratulated him on his lightning long-distance diagnosis of the son's appendicitis he hung his head modestly and muttered "An intelligent guess."

His wife shrunk visibly but not one of us noticed then.

He was an ENT man. A consultant in a hospital he would rather not name. Within the field of ENT his especial skill was in that last letter. He was a Throat man, he laughed. We could have no idea how fascinating and complicated throats were, that isthmus between the head and the rest of the body. He was probably right; as long as one tube sent the air down and the other pushed down the food and their paths didn't cross, we tended not to give the matter any thought. But then, there was The Voice, the most fragile and precious gift of evolution and it was the singer's voice that was the jewel in the human crown. His own voice dropped to a whisper and his prose dipped into purple.

It had been, on the face of it, a simple procedure. He had something like it to perform on almost every list. Simple nodules, yet his scalpel or his concentration or the steadiness of his nerve or muscle had failed for just that split second and a beautiful, wonderful soprano voice had been ruined, a huge career blighted, years of study, work and sacrifice reduced to nothing more than a small scar, and he felt responsible for the disaster. He could not be and would not be exonerated.

Who could not pity such a fall from grace and admire the moral courage to face it? We accepted his reminiscences about Laurence and Birgit and Cyril as the small treasures remaining to a man who had lost so much and if he chose to share them with us from time to time, the privilege was ours.

He and his wife moved to a flat just a little further out of town. We brought a champagne picnic to celebrate the move. He brought birthday presents for the sons full of sensitivity to their particular or even peculiar needs. He had a mild heart attack, his second, and we were as supportive as we could be to his frail, blonde wife, going to fetch her, taking her home, keeping her company whenever possible. He recovered, a little thinner, but once more sitting in his stall, selling small, interesting pieces, the best of their kind. When we moved upmarket to a new gallery on the other side of Oxford Street, Peter decided that he would move too. The quality of his stock, he had to concede, was devalued and out of place in Barrett Street.

I was struck a double blow, all on the same day. My husband had an abdominal abscess that burst on the operating table. My son fell out of the window at school. Ruth went daily to sit with my husband in St. John's Wood. I ran to Roehampton to sit with my son. The shop went into semi-hibernation. Rosemary, our staunch friend in need, helped beyond the call of friendship and duty. Ruth often managed to be in three places at once. I just tried to get from one day to the next. For advice I turned to Peter. Where should I go for a second opinion? Should I transfer my son from the national health to the private sector? A psychiatrist, perhaps, for my son, to help him deal with what had happened? What should I take to help me sleep but that would not reduce me to more of a zombie than I was already? Peter was at my side without stint. His wife suggested that perhaps I should seek some additional advice. Peter was full of quiet wisdom, giving me names and telephone numbers but asking me, sadly, not to quote him as the source of my information. It would be unseemly. I was moved by his tact.

I was too exhausted and bewildered to notice that the second opinions seemed elusive and that the psychologist who went to see my son, whom Peter had recommended for his youth and empathy, was still wet behind the ears and as nervous as a scalded cat. My son said he was tired of having to reassure him for fifty-five minutes a day.

The husband recovered. The son recovered. The marriage did not and there was Peter, this time an expert on all matters matrimonial.

It wasn't until Peter died, a couple of years later, having suffered a third heart attack, that we learned the meaning of the word "mythomane", translated into English more brutally as "compulsive liar". Once a medical student, he had never actually managed to qualify, though not for want of trying. His wife told us the story over tea and sympathy. She talked like someone shedding an impossibly heavy burden, pound by leaden pound.

"He was so completely convincing," she said flatly. "He romanced me out of a good job and a good life and convinced me that he could unhook the moon."

"Was he a gemmologist, at least?"

"Yes! That was about the only thing in his life that he really did and I've got the certificate to prove it."

Then she added, "Unless he printed it himself, of course."

"But how could you not tell me?" I shouted. "How could you not warn me?"

I shook with rage.

"I did try to warn you. I really did but I couldn't actually tell you. It wouldn't have been loyal."

Twenty-five years have passed and the rage has long gone. Ruth and I reminisce about him with sad warmth. He was so very much a part of those early days in our corner of Barrett Street market and he put all his lies and myths at our disposal with great kindness. We will never know how much he himself believed of the plot he was constantly weaving.

The owner of Barrett Street Antique Market was a skinny little East End Cockney with a beady eye and pointed shoes, a wheeler dealer who could have been an inspiration for a good television series. He walked round his domain, eyes darting, ready to pick up on some infringement of the house rules or, better still, looking if he could sell that nice little number lurking in the pocket of his coat to one of his captive tenants. His son presented a different image altogether. Tall, with a mop of curly hair, he was drop-dead handsome in unstructured Armani. He showed himself rarely in his Dad's slightly down-at-heel domain. He wheeled and dealt at a level which carries the more dignified label of "business transaction". He decided to open an antique gallery on the Mayfair side of Oxford Street, the stands to be an integral part of the gallery and not the shanty town that was Barrett Street. The passages were to be carpeted, the whole painted a somewhat lurid green much favoured by interior decorators aiming for a fresh, crisp effect; a colour that unless constantly renewed tends to stain and discolour much like a lettuce, with the same weary effect. But when we decided to make the move, the gallery was bright and beautiful. We put our names down for a room in the basement. This was easily four times larger than our Barrett Street stand so we were cross-examined by the gorgeous proprietor, his legs languidly stretched in front of him, as he looked down his aquiline nose at the paucity of our stock. A Book Room would give his gallery gravitas, but were we of the right quality? And were our books? We flashed a few books from our private collections, casually implying that these were random samples taken from endless shelves of treasures. He implied that we were in with a chance. We implied that it would be an incalculable loss to his kudos if we were not given our room. He liked kudos. We were awarded a year's lease. So we moved to pastures new, luminous, lettuce-green pastures.

Chapter 2 ½

The Day Books

As we go through the many years of day books, we realise that it is as much a record of the life of our bookshop as that of a friendship, and one that has survived the tensions of a partnership to boot.

It was a commonplace book with quotations from books we were enjoying. We sometimes had all too much time to read. Business was not always brisk. We dropped comments about our husbands, sons and mutual friends, which we will continue to hide between the covers of the diaries for the sake of discretion and libel. Ruth went in for aphorism in French. I wrote poems on sheets of paper which I tucked into the day books and which she collected and kept. On my sixtieth birthday she presented me with a bound copy of the poems.

We jotted down the wit of our customers, browsers, visiting lost souls and time wasters as well as our opinion of their wit and wisdom and sometimes dearth of soap. After all, this was our Day Book and the log of our lives as wives, mothers, friends, lovers, philosophers and booksellers. And sometimes the gossip curled the pages!

GOSSIP SONG (I)

Did you know?
Have they told you?
Have you heard?
Yes, it's hard to believe it,
It's ridiculous,
Absurd.
Why, she always seemed …
And he always looked …
But I thought you knew,
I thought you'd heard.

I don't want to be the first
Still, I think you ought to know,
Though it really isn't pleasant,
It will come as quite a blow,
I'm surprised you didn't notice,
I'm surprised it didn't show,
I'm surprised you haven't heard,
You didn't know.

I don't know how to put it,
How to tell you, what to say.
I'm your friend,
You're my friend
And a friendship can't betray.
Still, I'm surprised you didn't notice,
Why, you see them every day,
I'm surprised you haven't heard,
You didn't know.

Some wisdom and comments gathered at random:

"Do not think too much. Cela se voit sur le visage."
Instructions from one Glendale to another at a time of our lives when thinking was leaving visible scars. These have now mellowed into lines that define a lived-in face.

"We are commanded to forgive our enemies but you never read that we are commanded to forgive our friends."

"La solitude à deux. Il n'y a vraiment rien de mieux?"

Sometimes the wisdom was brought in by our customers and lingered on the premises for our delight.

What greater thoughtfulness and delicacy can there be than one lady asking another "How's the goldfish?"

"Much better, thank you," was the gracious reply.

I suppose that if it wasn't floating belly side up at the top of the tank, it must have been better but we were too discreet to enquire how she had made the diagnosis.

"What exactly do you collect?" she asked the young Dutchman who had asked to see several items in the top price bracket.

"Collect?" he said, puzzled. Then his face cleared.

"Profit," he said. "I am a dealer like you. Good to collect profit, no?"

One gentleman to another, both quite irate: "Sir, in this field, my opinions are facts."

The Day Book gives no clue as to the crop in this particular field.

Chapter 3

From Gray's to a shop of our own

We enjoyed the atmosphere of the market. The original sharp green glamour quickly settled into the slightly shabby comfort that is the lot of all antique markets, whatever fancy name they choose to call themselves, gallery, arcade, centre or even village. Above all, the years at Gray's gave us confidence. We had our room in the basement with enough shelf space to arrange our books into some semblance of order; children's books all together, illustrated books, our first etiquette books. We had a small glass case for miniature books and the fragile hand painted panoramas of Regent's Park and Crystal Palace. We had a desk and a chair for visitors. Our neighbours dealt in old lace, porcelain, jewellery and guns, mostly of good quality and attractive. The coffee bar was just round the corner from our room, so that a fresh sandwich, hot coffee and hot gossip were always to hand. Because we were in a room, however, we had an element of privacy. Tucked behind the desk we could sit quietly with a customer or with a friend and on rare occasions with each other; we manned "the shop" in turns. We had leisure to collate our books more carefully, to read our reference books, to study old catalogues. How fashions changed! In a catalogue of modern first editions published by a respectable bookseller in 1926, amongst the most expensive books offered were the novels of John Galsworthy. In 1976 they attracted hardly a flicker of interest even as reading copies.

From here we ventured to our first book fairs, at first tentatively as buyers on a small scale, then as exhibitors. We tried one or two book fairs in Brighton but quickly decided it was not a worthwhile effort for the amount of money taken and new contacts made. The best fairs were in Bath and in Oxford. Later we exhibited once a month in London. By the time we ventured abroad, we had learned to unpack, set up (Ruth's job) and be ready with hair brushed and smiles in place five minutes before the first rush of enthusiasts fell through the door. We learned how to pack up as quickly as possible, in total silence, at the end of a fair, and get our books to the car. We learned how to cry panic to the AA when the car broke down. Most important of all, we knew how to pick up a box of books, knees bent and back straight. To this day we pride ourselves on our ability to lift heavy objects without a twinge in the lower back, much to the admiration of grandchildren who expect more decrepitude.

At Gray's there were a lot more people ambling by than at Barrett Street, tourists from the plush Mayfair hotels close by, some who had strayed from the circuit of boutiques around Bond Street, enchanted by old lace, porcelain and jewellery. We rarely attracted a passing glance and when we did, it was followed by loud exclamations and questions impossible to answer.

"Why do you sell old books?"

"Do people actually buy these? For money?"

"They're quite nice but they're not exactly new, are they?"

"Are these real prices or just the prices for tourists?"

The professionals, the runners selling to their particular dealers, homed in on their contacts without a sideways glance. With time we had both runners and customers of our own who came to see us, perhaps with a sideways glance or two; there were some beautiful objects for sale around us.

We worked well. The quality of our stock improved as our knowledge and experience grew. We drew very little money in salary but ploughed our profit back into books. We had started off badly undercapitalised so over the years we generated our own capital through trade. It was certainly slower than a six-figure float would have been but it was much more satisfying. We began to talk about the possibility of the possibility of a shop. It would mean bigger overheads. Even in a good secondary position the rent would be high. Would we be able to keep the shelves stocked? We veered between worst-case scenario and manic optimism with very little in between.

And then we began to talk about it seriously. Our turnover would drop before it crept up again. How would we deal with insurance? Could we take a loan from the bank? To what extent should and could Monika and Ruth underwrite Glendale? We scribbled on the backs of envelopes and then transferred our calculations onto graph paper with different-coloured pens. The result looked businesslike enough but the resemblance to the map of the London Underground was not reassuring; the lower reaches of the Northern Line, in black, stood out forcefully and that was where we would be if our takings halved in the first twelve months.

We did not always see eye to eye. Ruth had an annoying amount of common sense where I felt fantasy and a gambler's streak was what was wanted. She thought that we should wait another couple of years. I wanted to go for it. We argued until I knew we should wait another couple of years and she thought we should go for it. We lurched from impasse to dead end. I left her a verse on the subject.

PLATFORM ONE

You keep your eyes
Option wide
So you cannot trip with me
When I fall under trains
Weighed down as you are
With all your incases
In cases

We stopped the courteous bickering and the artistic accountancy and decided we would fly this one on optimism, hard work and a few extra book fairs to make sure that there was always enough money in the bank to cover the fixed overheads. We would take a cut in our modest salaries; there would be time enough to enjoy the fat when we had some to enjoy.

And so, pointing to our healthy credit balance, we asked the bank manager to make a loan available should we need it. He wasn't entirely convinced that a shop was a good idea for two ladies but should we need it, really need it, he would allow us a small overdraft facility. For a limited period. With personal guarantees. To be reviewed monthly. As a particular favour in view of our long association with the bank. He handed out the ifs and buts, the handcuffs and the manacles in his flat, measured voice. Banking regulations, he explained, are there to protect the customer as much as the bank: the customer from his own stupidity and the bank from subsequent loss was the barely disguised implication. I wondered if the regulations had come down with Moses on a third tablet of stone; they were certainly more religiously adhered to than the conventional ten featured in Genesis. Bank managers were bred with a boredom chromosome. Were they as bored as they were boring? He tipped the balance. We were going to move into a shop to spike his obvious ill will.

We decided that the Marylebone area would be best for us. It was not far from our respective homes, just four stations down the Jubilee Line, and it was not too far from Gray's so that old customers would not have to trail across London to find us. The downside though was that it was not in an area full of interesting antiquarian bookshops. Both dealers and collectors like to "do" several shops in one day, especially those who have come from out of town or from abroad, so that if we were too far away from the known circuit, we would be left out. But then, Gray's was not on the traditional circuit and we had not suffered unduly. But then, Gray's was right next to an underground station. We took turns to play the devil's advocate. We both agreed, in the end, that we had to keep the stock interesting and give the prices an edge to keep our customers coming for more, even to Marylebone. Easy to say but always difficult to fulfil.

We found what we were looking for very quickly. That is, almost what we were looking for. The shop was modern and the rent was reasonable. There were shelves with bales of cloth which we emptied in our mind's eye and filled with books. The lighting was warm and welcoming. There was a large window which Ruth, with her talent for such things, would dress to the nines. The workshop was in the spacious basement and it was big enough for us to partition, so that we could have a section for cleaning and packing, with a corner for a small fridge and a kettle. And best of all, we would have our own lavatory and basin. At Gray's that particular facility had been the first to lose its designer appeal. On the other side of the partition there would be plenty of room for inexpensive second-hand books.

The tailors, father and son, who were selling the shop, showed us around, aware, surely, that Ruth and I had fallen a little in love with the place. On the walls were photographs of favourite customers, personalities we recognised from screen large and small, most prominently The Beatles. Their pictures were everywhere.

"Did you make their suits?" we asked, a little in awe of such proximity to the icons.

"Yes," said the father, with no further comment.

"And they come here?"

"Yes"

"Do you still make their suits?" True they were no longer The Beatles and one of them no longer lived in England, but still, big stars were traditionally loyal to the butcher, the baker and the candlestick maker who had looked after them before fame struck. It was part of the publicity underlining their solid moral values; we expected nothing less of The Beatles. The question was not answered. Father and son exchanged glances.

"And Brian Epstein?" I asked.

Again there was no reply but again, there was no photograph of Brian Epstein.

"Were they fun?" I went on, regardless of the stony silence, gazing at a photo of the four lads falling about laughing.

"That they were." said the son. Father looked at him sharply. And that was the end of that. We learnt no more. Where Messrs Lennon, McCarthy, Harrison and Starr have their clothes made, what are their favourite colours, what physical anomalies have to be compensated by expert cutting and tailoring, chest and inside leg measurements remained as closely guarded as any dictate of medical ethics or secrets of the confessional.

The big question mark that remained was the position of the shop. Because the block of flats it stood in had its main entrance in New Cavendish Street, the address of the shop, for some mysterious municipal reason, was registered as New Cavendish Street. But it wasn't. It was round the corner and you had to turn your head quite sharply to see it. Would we be allowed a neat little sandwich board on the corner to announce our presence? Would our old customers stomp up and down New Cavendish Street and when they could not find us, give up disgruntled? The shop itself was so attractive. There were four small armchairs there already, as if waiting for browsers. In our room at Gray's we turned away the second-hand books that we were offered and all but gave away the books that we had to buy in multiple lots in order to have the two or three we needed. Now we could have room for shelves of Adventure and Travel, Romance and Folly, Games, Players and Cheats, Science and Fiction. The ground floor would be serious, even scholarly. The lower ground floor would be the place where a serious browser would find the book he hadn't even realised he wanted.

Marylebone is an area full of doctors and their patients, lawyers and their clients so there would be passing trade of a different order because eventually they would turn their heads and spot us. We took the plunge.

When we took possession of the shop, all the signed photographs had, of course, gone. Many, many years later, those four little armchairs, recovered and restored to their full Art Deco glory, were given to Ruth's elder son. Now he has a son of his own, who perches on the red leather, and with rapt attention, plays a slightly simplified version of all the Beatles songs. It's enough to make one superstitious.

We moved into the shop on a Sunday, when it was possible to park the loaded cars outside the door without being harassed. The stacks of boxes grew until they blocked out the light. Sons helped. They fetched coffee and sandwiches and mountaineered over the boxes with whoops of glee. We, meanwhile, decided where to put the desk. Having already had some experience of theft, we worked out where to put the most valuable books and what could safely be displayed near the door. As we arranged the books, sons jumped on the empty boxes before piling them back into the cars. Their help was enthusiastic but sporadic. Inevitably. By Monday morning we were exhausted but more or less ready for business, a little sandwich board announcing our presence, wedged against the lamp post on the corner.

We continued to arrange and rearrange books on the shelves.
"Where are the books on the Communards?"
"Behind the Perrault."
"Silly of me. Where else would they be?"
Or else, "We've lost the box of valentines."
"You're sitting on it."
The usual snap and irritation of two very tired booksellers, hindered by helpful sons. We dusted, cleaned and labelled the shelves, completely

undisturbed by any potential customer. The odd passer-by glanced at Ruth's attractive window display and hurried on. In the middle of the afternoon the door finally opened and a representative from The Council walked in briskly and instructed us to remove our sandwich board which was a potential hazard and detrimental to the environmental quality of the area. Marylebone was not going to be turned into a slum by the likes of us, we were given to understand. He looked around him with distaste; obviously not a man for old books. Then a friend came in, looked around in her turn and admired the speed with which we had put the place together.

"Pity you're so tucked away here. Why don't you put one of those sandwich board things on the corner?"

We winced. And that was the end of the first day and it was not good.

The second day was much the same. Perhaps just a little more interest in the window display but not enough to provoke an enquiry. On the third day a man walked in and bought a book. He must have been a little astonished at the enthusiasm with which his purchase was wrapped, the transaction recorded on a suspiciously virgin page, and the ceremonious respect with which his small book was presented to him. But we had sold our first book in our own shop and the entry in the Day Book glowed with optimism and coloured ink.

Other customers followed as well as sitters who didn't even pretend to be customers, the light-fingered gentry, people with books to sell and friends who needed the lavatory and a little R & R. If all the world's a stage, so is a bookshop.

We certainly met some interesting people over the years. Ruth and I called them "Glendale People" as if they were a particular species, a bit odd and given to haunting our bookshop, or does a bookshop attract more customers on the lunatic fringe than, say, a greengrocer? Could it be that we were too sympathetic? We were certainly cheaper than a psychiatrist and less given to exacting prayer and penance than a priest.

We became hardened to being asked if we stocked envelopes and the Daily Mail. We denied vehemently that we had a lavatory and replied to any such request as if we had never heard of such a thing and had never been known to use one. Ever since the day that Ruth had walked in on a smart young man injecting himself with an illegal substance, sitting comfortably on our loo seat, we decided to use the place exclusively for our own convenience and to keep it locked.

The real problems seemed to arrive after 4 p.m., usually in the rain. You knew at once that they had no interest in books. A bookshop! Now there's sure to be someone in there with plenty of time on their hands who understands.

"Do you have a daughter?"

"No, I haven't."

"Lucky."

The small woman pulled books off the shelves and rammed them back almost without a glance. She wore crumpled trousers and murky trainers, as if she had crossed much rough terrain to get to us. The two uneven furrows between her brows were carved. Her eyes were fierce. I tried to take refuge in paperwork but the sound of my stock culling the brunt of her wrath kept me alert.

Her pinched face hovered over mine, daring me to look up and give her some attention. I resisted. She banged two books on the desk in front of me. I conceded defeat.

"I have," she said.

"What?" I asked, all distracted inattention.

"A daughter," she snapped, "and she's in love."

"Very nice."

That was it! Two bland words I should not have said. The dam burst and the horrors of the love affair spilled over the shop. He was rude. Foul-mouthed. Dirty. Treated her daughter badly. Maybe even slapped her about. Anybody in their right mind could see that he wasn't right in the head. Only her daughter couldn't see it. Wouldn't see it. Cried. Couldn't work. Wouldn't listen. Oh, the misery of it.

I kept very still, hoping that no sympathetic twitch of an eyebrow would unleash more of this domestic drama.

"Shall I wrap the books up for you?" I asked when the tide of words had abated just a little.

She looked at the books with disdain. "What on earth for?"

She stormed out of the shop outraged by my impertinence.

The next visit was also in the early evening. She told me that the lover had moved in. Things were beginning to disappear from the house. Nobody in the family was willing to help her, least of all her sister. Her sister was very busy and very, very famous. If I knew who her sister was I would be amazed. I peered at the troubled little face for some shadow of resemblance to anyone so amazingly famous that even I couldn't fail to know her. Meryl Streep? Margaret Thatcher? No. All I could see was a Yorkshire Terrier with sinusitis. Of course, her sister never hesitated to call on her whenever her help was needed and she always gave it unstintingly. I wondered what so famous a sister would need by way of help; perhaps someone to snap at the ankles of intruders. She bought a book for a modest £3.50 which she tucked into the depths of her great bag for safekeeping.

When I saw her crossing the road to come into the shop some weeks later, I grabbed a pile of catalogues and hid in glazed concentration. I did not look up when she came in.

"Do you have anything about the law?" she whispered.

"What sort of law?"

"He won't move out." she said.

"Well, we have one or two books written for the layman downstairs," I said doubtfully. "but don't you think you should get some proper advice?"

She looked at me blankly.

"I can't afford to do that anymore."

I knew that there was advice to be had without fees, even from the police, but we had learnt not to put our oar into unknown waters. She left her great bag next to my desk and went downstairs, to appear some twenty minutes later carrying every book which might have some bearing on her problem, however remotely.

As I wrapped the books, I glanced at the weary woman, barely five feet tall, and I couldn't help wondering about the daughter who had invited so much havoc into her mother's life.

"How about your daughter?" I asked.

"My daughter can't stand the sight of him any more. She's gone to Wales to stay with friends until the coast is clear."

I laughed. It was difficult not to.

"Well, at least she has come to her senses. You'll see, everything will be fine." I produced my soothing cliché.

"Nonsense," she snapped. "She can't come to what she hasn't got and everything isn't going to be fine with that lout in the house."

"I'm sure he'll leave with a little pressure and meanwhile your daughter has learnt her lesson. The young can be so thoughtless."

My stock of soothing clichés was rich. She looked with pity at my complete incomprehension.

"My daughter is thirty-two," she said quietly, "and my daughter does not learn."

I shut the door of the shop behind her and reflected with great tenderness on my mob of unruly sons.

Besides the woman with the sister so famous that we would be knocked sideways if we were ever to discover her identity, which we never managed to do, we did have many famous faces come through the door. Most famous faces we recognise from newspapers and television so it is always startling to be confronted by a face that has a body and that the whole is three-dimensional and of normal size. On the whole, we gave no more than a little nod of recognition and let them look at the books in peace. Actors, even film stars, were easy to recognise. Dustin Hoffman liked an old, illustrated copy of Hamlet and read a great deal of it to his wife and to me, our own command performance. Some of the household names from TV soap operas looked vaguely familiar and we always made sure that they knew that they were recognised without giving away that we couldn't put a name to them to save our souls. If they wanted to order a book or asked to do a search, we would slide the index card across the desk and ask them to fill it out themselves, "in lieu of an autograph"; we have been known to simper. Actors, we discovered, were fragile and a little rub of the ego was always appreciated.

Paul Daniels walked in and asked if we had any Victorian boxes of conjuring tricks. We did! There were two or three tucked away in the basement; since we did not know if the jumbles of feathers and mirrors, eggs and chains were complete, we did not know how to price them, so I brought them all up and he proceeded to show us how the links could all be joined into a chain and then split up again into links. He did it twice, inches away from our noses and we could still not see how it was done. He explained why this trick was incomplete as he put eggs together and took them apart again; the fluffy chick in the middle was missing but who cared? Feathers came and went, silk handkerchieves appeared from empty tubes. There were two other people in the shop and we gathered round, peered up his sleeves but still he was faster than four pairs of eyes and he was delighted by our amazement. He asked the price of all three boxes. I pulled a modest sum out of the hat. He paid. I put out my hand for the note. It disappeared. I looked startled. He looked blank.

"May I have my change?" he asked sweetly. He held out his hand.

It was my turn to look blank.

"I'm sorry," I muttered, "I'm not quite sure ..."

"it's in the drawer." He laughed.

I opened the drawer and there was a crisp note on top of the day book.

I gave him his change, very carefully, still not sure if I had slipped the note into the drawer without thinking or if this had been the last conjuring trick before Mr Daniels left, laughing.

The man in the dark suit and the clerical collar was delightful. He had a strong foreign accent, Italian or maybe Spanish and he wanted first editions of detective novels, talking about Miss Marple and Lord Peter as if they were old, dear friends. He sat and talked for a while. He had a way of wrapping personal questions so adroitly that I found myself saying more, and more frankly, than I would ever dream of doing to a total stranger. It is so easy to relax one's guard when an elderly man with an Uncle Holly smile appears to find your life and opinions interesting.

"Your collar announces your calling." I said. "You must be very good at the pastoral side of your work."

I was a little resentful that I had fallen so neatly into what I considered a trap.

"I do my best." he replied gently.

We got down to the serious business of his "wants" list. He was a serious collector.

"Now, if you would be good enough to let me have your name, address and a contact number, we will let you know as soon as we have found something that might interest you."

"Ah," he said, "the contact number is not so easy. I am not always available. You see, I am something called a cardinal ... You know what is cardinal?"

My general knowledge stretched to cardinal.

When King Constantine walked in I am afraid I giggled. He was most definitely three-dimensional and lese-majesty dishy. I find the word "sir" difficult to pronounce as a matter of form; Nobel prize-laureate, certainly, the issue of royal loins, certainly not. So, I gave him a kind of half cough by way of greeting. He told me what he was looking for and assumed that I knew who he was because he gave me the name and address of his ADC for further contact. We were more comfortable with ADCs.

And slowly, over the years, by word of mouth, we became a part of local life. People came to buy original presents for birthdays and for christenings.

"Such fun!"

"Quite charming!"

"I'm sure there was a set of these in the old nursery in Hampshire!"

They prattled and cooed and were delighted whilst we learnt not to wince. At Christmas they bought Victorian Christmas cards and at the beginning of February they came for Victorian valentines overwrought with putti and garlands of blue forget-me-nots. We became a social centre. We did not attract London's intellectual crème, no comparison with Shakespeare & Company implied, but in our own lowly way we became a hub of rest and recreation for the tired and the lonely and the bored of Marylebone. Not all Glendale people were slightly batty.

Mrs Apfel was the widow of a surgeon and lived in a mews house round the corner from the shop. She wore hat and gloves at all times, felt or straw, fine leather or cotton, according to season. She never sat back in the chair next to the desk, just perched on the edge, as if to underline that she only had a few minutes to spare and that she was sparing them entirely for my benefit. For some reason she avoided Ruth but then, Ruth had accumulated her own clientele of sitters. I was her choice as depository for all the talents and moral superiorities of her late and constantly lamented husband who should have been awarded a Nobel prize in at least three categories, if the prize committee had known its business. Her duty now was to keep as busy and useful as she had been during his lifetime, so she divided her day into specific segments and filled each segment to its last ordained minute. There was house-cleaning with ten minutes allowed for coffee. There was one hour for the newspaper because an educated person had to keep abreast of the times, its politics and literature. Mrs Apfel had an excellent memory for expert opinions and read book reviews rather than books. Lunch was a sandwich. Fifteen minutes. Then there was a walk which included buying provisions for the evening meal, to include green vegetables and meat no more than three times a week. Her dear husband never ate meat more than three times a week. Popping into our shop was a permitted break in her constitutional walk and shopping expedition. Her conversation allowed for no curiosity about my life or my husband or our shop. No, when not reminiscing about the giant of a man who had been her husband, she went over the minutiae of her daily life, reassuring herself along the way that she was doing well, not frittering away the day, that she would be able to give him a good account of herself when at last he greeted her, his perfectly tuned harp in hand. She wondered if she should take up some new activity to keep her mind alert. He would certainly not have approved of cards. Learning a new language would be an excellent project except that after a certain age, it had to be admitted, the brain's glue was less efficient and vocabulary did not stick; she had tried French. She wondered if she could permit herself a couple of hours a day, towards the early evening say, when all the day's exigencies had been fulfilled, of self indulgence.

I asked myself wryly if this might, perhaps, include a little reading and even the purchase of a book or two but I kept the question to myself. There was something admirable about the old lady struggling against the current of loneliness and bereavement on a lifebelt of self-imposed obligations. I agreed that she might take up something a little frivolous since she had spent so much of her life in intellectual activity (she glowed) and had she thought of doing some handwork? Pottery? Jewellery? Weaving? She had not but the idea appealed. In due course, Mrs Apfel took up painting in oils, with classes at the local institute. In due course she rearranged her schedule, allowing herself three generous segments a week to paint at home, as well as her class on Thursday. With no modesty, false or genuine, she announced that she had talent. And in due course I was invited to tea.

I did not wear hat or gloves but with a good suit, a fine leather handbag and my shoes well polished, I felt I was doing her honour. There were two easels in the room, one next to the window held the work in progress and one facing the dining area displayed the work she wished her visitor to view. For my pleasure, she had put up a painting of a bridge over a river, with ornate street lamps, something between the Pont Alexandre III in Paris and the Charles Bridge in Prague, painted in solid black. The river, the bridge and the lights emanating from the black lamps were screened behind a general blur of pinkish fog. The overall effect was curiously pretty, Mrs Apfel's lack of drawing skills nicely camouflaged by dabs of pastel colours. It was obvious that she had enjoyed painting it.

"You are having fun." I said warmly.

"Fun?" I caught the edge of indignation in her voice.

"Well, you have certainly taken up something that gives you pleasure," I pointed to the window and the work in hand. "You enjoy your painting."

"I have found my vocation. Mr S. has compared my work to Monet."

Mr S. was her instructor at the institute. I could see some affinity in the subject matter, certainly, but to push the comparison beyond that was not fair to either. Was Mr S. indulging the harmless vanity of a new pupil or had Mrs Apfel misheard or misunderstood some well-intentioned encouragement?

"Did he?" I asked weakly and hid my face behind a tea-cup.

"Oh, yes," she said with all the seriousness of the guardian of an immense talent, overwhelmed by the responsibility to nurture it. She sighed as if wearied by the burden.

"Now, my dear, you will have to forgive me, but I will not be able to come in and keep you company in the shop any more. I'm simply not going to have the time. I hope to have enough work ready for my first exhibition by October, somewhere nice in Cork Street, I think, and it is going to take all my time, every minute of it. I'll let you know in plenty of time and of course you shall have an invitation."

She was as good as her word. She did not come into the shop again, not even to tell me how she was getting on. October came and went without any invitation.

Very soon after moving into the shop, we realised that we could not quite manage on our own. We had to buy as well as sell and the demands of home had to be met. When Ruth first came to England, she met the small, tight-knit circle of her husband's childhood friends and it was their wives and girlfriends who eased her into her new English life. Fifty years on, the circle remains unbroken, even though two families have gone to live in Canada. One of the then fiancées was Rosemary.

She had worked for many years as personal assistant to a captain of industry. It is difficult to know if she learned to be organised and supremely tactful in the course of her working life or she had come to the job with those qualities already deeply ingrained. In either case, it was Glendale who reaped the benefit. At about the time that we decided to move from our Book Room at Gray's to a shop of our own, Rosemary decided that she wanted to change direction, so she gave in her notice and took on some voluntary work in an old people's home whilst she pondered what to do next. Given her personality, in no time at all she was working as hard with as much responsibility as she had had in her well-paid full-time job. But if you only know how to work full tilt, you work full tilt. She agreed to work one day a week for us, so we had Rosemary Wednesdays and organised as much of our buying trips and auction-viewing around that day.

Soon enough, we had gentlemen poking their heads round the door with that casual, throw-away question "Rosemary not here today, then?"

So as well as Rosemary Wednesdays, we had Rosemary gentlemen and it was no use trying to show them books on a Ruth or Monika Thursday.

Three is not just an odd number, it is a difficult one. In spite of her long-standing friendship with Ruth, however, she kept a certain professional detachment. She didn't take sides; she could be equally exasperated with us both. From time to time she had to put on a blue beret and become a one-woman Peace Corps, when Ruth and I locked horns. Fortunately it did not happen that often but in a long working partnership, clashes happened. She was very good at negotiation, arbitration and throwing a bucket of cold water when all else failed.

Given enough notice, Rosemary could be relied on to man the shop when we had major book fairs, important auctions that clashed, so that Ruth and I had to go in different directions to cover them and, of course, holidays.

Over and above Glendale, Ruth and I were friends, the boys got on just fine, and for many years we rented a house together by the sea for the summer holidays. Now, why is a close loving friendship between two women so difficult to accept without a suspicious little cough? Yet for years we did not hear it; it had never occurred to us to listen for it. Then, we had an enquiry phrased in a way that confirmed that all those smiles and innuendoes were smiles of complicity, nudge, nudge, wink, wink.

"Why do you have two telephone numbers on your card?"
"Because we have two homes."
"What on earth for?"

"Do you have anything by Radclyffe Hall?"
"Well of Loneliness. It's a first but not a particularly good copy."
"Nothing else?"
"Fraid not."
"I was wondering who to ring. Then I thought if anybody would have something for me, you two would."

Ruth put down the receiver, bemused.

We are a nosey, gossipy lot in the book business and this was not the first time it had been assumed that ours is more, much more than a good business relationship and a firm friendship. Between us, we have five sons, three husbands (not concurrently) and several discreet staging posts along the way but somehow the perception remained that we were gay.

In fact, we often encountered disappointment when the truth could no longer be ignored. My stepson, who is gay and who has chosen to live in a Holland where he can lead an open life, maintains that the book trade must have a rare, communal attitude. He envies us. My view is a little more cynical; could it be that it is difficult to accept that two women can remain in partnership for over twenty years with nothing more to bind them than affection and a love of books?

When Rosemary, slim, neat, dressed with impenetrable formality during working hours, became well known to our colleagues as a member of the team, the confusion must have been, well, confusing.

Rosemary continued to give most of her spare time to running the haven for old, tired and retired refugees. A year or two after Mrs Apfel had told me that she would no longer have time to visit me in the shop, I went to a bazaar organised by Rosemary in the home, to raise money for necessary maintenance.

Sitting in a corner of the garden, wearing white gloves and a splendid straw hat, was Mrs Apfel. I asked Rosemary how long she had been there.

"A few months now. She is very quiet, doesn't really mix with the other residents."

"And does she still paint?"

"No, I don't think so. She does talk as if she and Monet were related, but no, she doesn't paint."

A couple of years later, Glendale acquired another lady helper, inadvertently confirming, perhaps, the presence of a lesbian cell in Marylebone.

Eugenia was not her real name, but her tall, stately bearing seems to call for some imperial alias. She used to pop into the shop. She lived locally, just a small flat, and always had ten minutes to spare to look out for a good second-hand book in the basement, where she could find a hardback for a couple of pounds. She didn't like paperbacks. They didn't feel like proper books. Her quick ten minutes soon became twenty and then an hour.

"Here, I am so tall I can reach that for you. No need to get the steps."

"Let me hold that for you."

"I am going downstairs anyway, so I'll take that box down with me."

Before we had quite realised what had happened, she was part of the team. She left her phone number on the desk just in case there was ever an emergency; no need to shut the shop and run because she would babysit with pleasure, and with all our growing boys veering between chickenpox and disasters on the rugby pitch, inevitably the dreaded call came from the school matron and within ten minutes Eugenia was there, complete with Thermos flask. She was perfect. Too discreet to open the day book, she had messages, calls and takings tabulated on a separate sheet, with the time of the call marked to the nearest minute - Mr Smith called in at 11.32 a. m. and Mr Brown telephoned at 14.27 p. m. - and the receipts complete with time of transaction and cheque number. She had been somebody's irreplaceable personal assistant and this was the way she had always done things, the right way, with no leeway for ambiguity.

Eugenia's happiest years had been during the war, she admitted apologetically, when, in her smart uniform, she had enjoyed the comradeship and complicity of doing important war work and the nights she had danced away. "A Good Time Girl!" she said and it was easy to imagine the raw-boned girl, a generous glass of gin and it in her hand, laughing raucously among pale RAF boys.

On Thursdays she wasn't available because her friend came on Thursdays. He came every week and brought his dirty shirts. She made him lunch and gave him the previous week's batch washed, pressed and folded. She had met him towards the end of the war, a doctor, married and gorgeous. She still blushed when she mentioned how tall and handsome and irresistible he had been. She had not even tried to resist him. From the beginning she had accepted that divorce was out of the question because his wife was an invalid, perhaps mentally ill, that was never quite clear, but only a cad would abandon a sick wife and he was anything but that. So they met when they could and built dreams of a future together in an old country cottage. They went to estate agents and viewed what was on offer. She had always wanted beams but they were both so tall that they were sure to bump their heads before they got used to it. They had had picnics in Sussex and stolen the odd week-end in the West Country. Gloucestershire was full of the kind of cottage they both wanted and when the time was right, they would have no trouble finding one, not too far from a market town but nowhere too touristy, and as banal as it sounded, she wanted roses round the door. She sat next to the desk, nursing her mug of tea and dreamed aloud, thirty years of dreaming undiminished and unfaded.

Of course, his children knew about her and loathed her, which she supposed was the reason that he only came once a week now. He was much older than she was, nearly eighty, and they kept an eye on him. She did not talk about him often but when she did there was a breathless girlishness about her and for all that she was at least twenty years our senior, it was difficult not to feel older, wiser and cynical, but there was no room for the least hint of our reality in her fairy tale. She had worked hard all her life and her little flat was her own. Once they were established in the country she might let it or they might use it as a pied-à-terre so that they could come up to London for the theatre and concerts and she could keep a couple of her nice frocks in town.

We had known her for a couple of years when one afternoon she came into the shop, white, and sat down heavily. The phantom wife was no more. She was dead. Soon, very soon now, it would be her turn to have a life and a home and walk openly down the street at his side. Except that he was now eighty. He had lived and worked in his dark, Victorian house in South London for over fifty years and he was not going to move. He was sorry to disappoint her. He half-heartedly invited her to move in with him but that would mean exposing herself to regular doses of venom from his children and she had her pride. They had planned to live in a cottage in the country when he was free. He was free. Surely now, at last, all those years of love and patience would be rewarded and all those plans and picnics and promises would materialise into a cottage with beams and roses round the door. Then, one Thursday, he did not come. Panic-stricken she ran to the shop because she wanted to ring with one of us there. A woman answered the phone and told her that he never wanted to see her or to speak to her again. His daughter had been worried about Eugenia's influence on her father. She had had visions and nightmares and had sent a friend of hers, a clairvoyant, to sort out the problem. The clairvoyant had told him that Eugenia was an evil spirit incarnate, a witch who had cast a spell over his wife and that was the reason she had never recovered from her illness. Eugenia had killed her.

"But how can he believe such a thing?" she whispered. "He's a doctor, an educated man. It's not possible, not possible. How could he believe that of me?" But he did. Or he used it as an excuse not to be molested by outdated dreams of country cottages and beams and roses round the door.

"Not possible." she muttered regularly. She continued to come and help but somehow her light had dimmed. She lost weight very rapidly. She said that she did not feel up to the mark but she came more often for all that. And then she did not come any more. We telephoned. She was scrupulously polite and thanked us for our concern but no, she would prefer us not to visit and no, she did not need anything, her neighbour was helping her out and she was sure that she would soon be feeling better. We rang several times and the response was always the same except that each time she was just a little more impatient. We were a nuisance, disturbing her. She had turned her face to the wall.

Neither of us read the sort of novel where the heroine, rejected and abandoned, dies of a broken heart. Too far-fetched, they are usually badly written and the covers are lurid. Yet here, just off Marylebone High Street, without crinoline or smelling salts but rather in lambswool and sensible shoes with plenty of wear in them, skilled in double-entry bookkeeping, an elderly woman was dying of a broken heart. And the villain was an old doctor, too old and tired to realise her stale dreams.

Eugenia died within the year.

Chapter 3 ½

People seem to be able to leave a shoe shop or a dress shop without making a purchase and without qualm. Not so a bookshop. There seems to be some compulsion to seek absolution but then, perhaps books really are sacred and not to buy one is a sin. So an excuse has to be given and here are just a few that we jotted down.

"I don't normally buy books."
"No?"
"Do you sell these kids' books then?"
"Yes."
"Great, aren't they?"
"Yes."
"Must buy a book some time."
"What for?"
"Don't know really. Perhaps I won't bother then."
And he didn't.

"Do you sell bookends?"

Well, suppose one has to start somewhere.

"Do you sell diaries?"
"No, we're not that kind of a bookshop."
"Well, I only wanted a small one."

"I like them, but I am not sure that my interior decorator will approve."

"It's not really what I had in mind. Do you have anything a bit newer?"

"I quite like it but it's got too many pictures."
A sad indictment of a book illustrated by Arthur Rackham.

"But it's foreign! I can't read foreign."

"I was looking for a third edition."
Faint hope of finding a copy; the book never went beyond a small first edition.

"Can I use your loo?"
Direct and no double dealing. He did not come into the shop to mess about buying books.

"I'll buy it if you come and read it to me as my bedtime story."
Wink, wink. Nudge, nudge. No sale.

"I won't have any leather binding in the house. I am a vegetarian."
A woman of principle, wearing red rubber wellies.

"My daughter never reads a book, so I want to buy her one for her twenty-first birthday."
"Isn't that a little unkind?"
"Unkind! What kindness can she expect? I told you. She doesn't read." He exploded.
In truth, what greater filial impiety can there be?

"I see that you have an interesting shelf on Manners and Morality. Would you have anything on how to conduct an affair when married?"
"Would that be from the point of view of manners or morality?"
A long, contemplative pause.
"Manners, I think."
We found nothing in stock.

Un bel'italiano came in, cashmere jacket draped over shoulders, and asked for something with a beautiful binding to decorate his drawing room, contents of no significance. We simply had nothing bello enough. He should have stood there himself for more decorative it is difficult to imagine, contents of no significance.

He stood in the middle of the shop and looked around him very slowly.
"I want to buy a present for a friend."
"What sort of book do you think your friend might like?"
"Oh, I don't want to buy him a book!"
We had so little else to offer other than our fixtures and fittings.

"Why do you sell books?"
With the politest of smiles she replied, "Why do you buy books?"
"I don't."

... and a cry from the heart when too many excellent reasons were offered in the course of a single day.

BOOKSELLER'S BLUES
(with respectful apologies to W. H. Auden and his sad Roman soldier.)

Leather needs waxing. Cloth's covered in dust.
Architecture's crumbling. Law's turned unjust.

Biography, History, Adventure to spare.
Sixteen stacks in the basement. Don't anyone care?

We sell Art to the Gentry, Peter Rabbit to kids,
Romance to the lonely, still trade's on the skids.

There's a shelf of morocco, gilt titles, raised bands,
incunabules, huge folios that you hold in both hands.

Twenty volumes of Dickens, in fine mottled calf,
And a rare early Auden, with a signed epigraph.

There are books topographic, from France to Brazil
And a yard of Sir Walter that's lingering still.

Old German erotic discreetly on view,
Letched by the many, bought by the few.

Glazed boards, illustrations, aquatint, pochoir, line,
Philosophy, science, moral, divine,

Out of print, out of favour, we serve every need.
In the mid-1990s, doesn't anyone read?

Chapter 4

On being women in the book trade

He ambled in, measured my hips with an expert eye.
"Who collects this sort of thing?"
"Collectors." I said.
He raised an eyebrow and left to start his collection elsewhere.

When we were in Barrett Street and afterwards in Gray's, we had no particular reason to notice that we were young women and therefore not quite competent. Once in a shop of our own we found that we were asked a little too often at what time the boss would be in and would it be possible to have a word with Mr Glendale. A woman selling books in an upmarket antique gallery is assumed to be an amateur. An antiquarian bookshop assumes expertise and knowledge.

On the train back from Paris one evening I ran across one of our colleagues, a young man who had been in the trade no longer than we had.

"Been doing a little shopping, dear?" he asked kindly.

The "dear" grated like chalk on a blackboard.
"Actually," I drawled, "I'm coming back from luncheon at the Elysée."
His jaw dropped. A lie, to be effective, should be a whopper.

No, being a woman in the book trade was not all silk endpapers and dentelles. No, there is no great wail of complaint ahead because on the whole we did well.

Go to any book fair and you will see that we are admirably represented and established. It just takes longer. Look around the same book fair and see how many young women there are, as opposed to young men, excluding the brave souls who make the sandwiches and fill the Thermos flasks, lend a sturdy back during the setting up and then sit patiently reading The Guardian whilst their bookdealin' man goes off book dealing.

As we grew older, with reading glasses perched on the end of our noses, we were allowed a little authority. There was a young man, later an established member of the trade, whose early efforts were greeted with wonder and admiration. The world of books had produced its own prodigy. Our efforts were regarded with much the same amazement as were women preachers by Dr Johnson.

At a New York Book Fair, a renowned colleague picked up an early children's book from our glass showcase.
"You know it's a second edition, don't you?"
"Yes, we do."
"You know it has two more illustrations than the first, don't you?"
"Yes, we do."
"The first edition was not coloured."
"Yes, we know."
He looked at us with contented disbelief. All the information, and more, was neatly written on a card which he had pushed to one side when he had taken out the book, but how could he have guessed that we were capable of so much research? He put the book back in the showcase, well pleased with his own generosity. He had passed on these little crumbs from his great store of knowledge and thus lightened our darkness.
We weren't proud. We sought crumbs, whole loaves in fact when our research failed us, and it was given without stint. Nevertheless, would this venerable colleague have presumed that a man could have, would have

brought an item of great value to a major international fair and not have done just a smidgin of homework first? This was not an isolated incident, merely an example of many that made us gnash our teeth and weep into our tea.

We have a list of remarks, gathered over the years, that would chip the confidence of the sturdiest lady bookseller.
"Odd sort of job for a girl. Still, I don't suppose you need any qualifications."

"Wouldn't you prefer to work with something pretty? No? Strange."

"You do know what a percentage is, don't you?"

"I'm looking for a first edition in its original covers. I think I'd better explain what that is."

"Who does all the paperwork for you?"

"Can't you get a nice man to keep you, a nice looking girl like you? This is no sort of job."

Then, there was the man who slapped a fifty-pound note on the desk as payment for a book marked at £80. He didn't say a word, just stared defiantly. Following his example of negotiation through mime, I put the book back on the shelf. That did provoke a reaction.
"Good God, woman, how do you expect to run a business? Have you never heard of a turnover? Of cash flow? You'd better get somebody to teach you the basic rudiments of business."

We had to admit that women customers, when really unpleasant, can be far, far worse than men. One of us could be sitting behind the desk, facing the entrance to the shop, with a man tucked in at the side, even to the untutored eye not in the captain's chair, yet many a woman will inevitably come in and address her question to the back of the male head rather than to the female face looking up at her, bright-eyed and ready to be of service.
There is also a whole sub-species of women who have cultivated a special manner of address to other women working in shops. Never once

have I felt this vague, insolent disdain from a man. It is difficult to contain in words. Rejected books are handed back without a word and without looking up. Our lady customer will demand the price of this and point to the books she wants brought for her inspection while she sits herself firmly in your place behind the desk. She will tell you for which of her brilliant children and renowned relatives she is buying presents, all with a superior sneer as if you, poor cow, had arrived in the world through parthenogenesis in order to be free to serve her without the distraction of other loyalties. She scorns any information you may offer and dictates terms. She sails out of the shop leaving hours of work behind her. Can a woman be a misogynist?

This sort of experience has made us sensitive in John Lewis and courteous at the check-out desk in the supermarket. Rejected skirts are replaced neatly on their hangers. Trolleys are loaded swiftly with due care to the number of carrier bags we take. Salesladies are subjected to the full beam of our grateful smiles.

With the passage of time, the explosions in the Day Books grew less common. Perhaps our skin grew thicker and the bouquet of arrogant ladies less irritating. Perhaps we were taken more seriously.

Of course there are advantages to being a woman in the book trade. There always have been. When we find a book for a customer who has been searching for months or even years, we are often rewarded with flowers, chocolates, apple strudel and, on one occasion, four piping hot chips in a paper bag. I doubt if many of our male colleagues are so handsomely treated. We have had all manner of proposals, propositions and compliments, not every single one to do with the buying or selling of books. On one or two occasions, we have got away with murder, only because we are women. We have laughed often, cried once or twice, and been kept on our toes at all times.

Looking round at the careers of our friends, we think we have had the best of it. We have travelled, met the strangest people (only the customers, nothing strange about our fellow booksellers of any gender) and infiltrated musty attics and stately homes. Because we are women, little old ladies, of whom there seem to be a great many in Marylebone, were not afraid to ask us round to look at their fathers' books. As a member of the ABA, a credential I flaunted, I have been allowed to examine books in the museum in Parma that normally never leave their showcase. As a lady member and therefore to be trusted (I've never worked out the logic of this, but it was not in my interest to question the curator) I was left alone with them unsupervised.

We started as tadpole booksellers almost twenty-five years ago. It has been bumpy. Yet this must be the best job in the world for a woman. And to the booksellers who told us to go home and mind the babies all those years ago, well Glendale has five of them, all grown to manhood healthy and strong among the bookshelves.

Ruth and I set a timetable and tried to keep to it. We each had our regular days, whether in the antique market or later in the shop and when Rosemary joined us, Wednesday became Rosemary Day. It made it possible to balance work and the running of our homes, to plan holidays, view auctions, freeze at sons' football matches and even have the occasional lunch with a friend. When we went off to book fairs, Rosemary took over altogether. When the sons grew older and had the first shadow of a moustache as evidence that we were not using forced child labour, they sometimes helped out, babysat the shop for a morning or an afternoon. They even got paid. They were left a clean sheet of paper or two and a nice sharp pencil with which to make notes. And the message that Ruth and I left for each other before a son took over was always

"Don't Forget to Lock it Away."

Censorship, certainly. The Day Books were our uncensored line of communication and not mete for young men with fluffy facial hair to read, especially not if the young men were sons. Not then, perhaps not even now. There was too much soul searching, pain, unseemly advice and unmaidenly humour, quite unsuitable for sons.

We each had a short line of gentleman callers, for the most part genuine customers who drew out the pleasure of looking at books by an extra ten minutes of light-hearted conversation with an attractive young woman, nothing more. There were, inevitably, one or two whose wives didn't understand them but our sympathy was never quite strong enough to draw us out of the shop, not even for coffee and cake in Marylebone High Street. We became quite efficient at little nods and platitudes. It was only when for some good reason we altered the timetable, did we realise that the gentleman callers were in two distinct teams; Ruth and I were not interchangeable. The disappointment when they came in and found the wrong one sitting behind the desk was barely disguised and sometimes not disguised at all.

"She not here then today?"

"She?"

"The other one."

"No. May I help you?"

Here, the replies came in all shapes and sizes, from the diffident to the aggressive.

"No, no. It's all right. Really. She was looking out for a book for me and I just wondered ... you know."

Or: "No. I don't think so. Will she be in later?"

Or even, in the worst case, "Certainly not!"

They often appear in the Day Book identified by a single initial and, sad to say, for the most part we can no longer put a name or a face to them.

"A. came in looking for you. Did not find you. Even went downstairs to see if you were lurking there. Left without saying 'Good bye' ".

"G. came in with coffee and buns for you. 'Delighted to share them with you of course.' Bad liar that one. Buns delicious."

"Tall, thin and bald. All yours. Would not leave his name."

"P. came in and would not believe me when I said you weren't here. Very rude. So I looked under the desk and in the petty cash box and when I still didn't find you he left in a huff."

"Your schoolmaster came and has left you a gift of Greek poetry. C16., 12mo, vellum. In Greek. Enjoy."

And then a tall thin man walked in. To say that he was handsome was an understatement. He made no show that he had come in to find a book. He did glance at me, it's true, but failed to notice whether I was fish or fowl.

"Ruth not here?" he asked with a Scottish lilt.

"I'm afraid she's not. May I help you?" I asked. It was the standard polite question but I knew I couldn't.

"Thank you, no," was the polite answer and he left without further question or further explanation.

"WHO was that?????" I wrote in the Day Book and underlined the question till there was a hole in the page.

She wrote back one word. His name. I asked no further questions and she gave no explanations.

There is no need to look to Tolstoy to measure the quality of unhappiness. All marriages that break down, whether slowly or fast, have become unhappy; that is the only constant. The rupture itself, when it arrives, causes more grief and anger with ripples the size of tidal waves engulfing family and close friends. Ruth's marriage broke down. Later so did mine. We propped each other up and Glendale held us together. With all the wisdom of hindsight sifted and resifted over many years, perhaps each of us may have acted and reacted differently. But we were in younger, angrier mode then.

Ruth and her husband separated, she and her boys had moved into a flat. However civilised a separation, and hers had been civilised enough, though not initially amicable, there were wounds to lick and scars to grow, a different routine to establish, a new sort of life to cobble together. The Thin Scot courted. He was patient. She was tempted. He stepped forward. She slid back. There were the boys to consider. It was all too fresh. This was merely the need for comfort, the famous rebound. He avoided pressure. She edged forward sideways like a wily crab. I watched, observed, encouraged and reassured. Her ability to argue herself out of any sort of decision was amazing and went on for months. She wasn't playing cat and mouse, not because she didn't like games that young, attractive women play, but because this was not the time in her life to play anything.

He asked her out to dinner.

"I've been out to dinner. Thank you."

He asked her out to lunch.

"I've had lunch several times. But thank you."

He asked her to the theatre.

"There's nothing I particularly want to see. Thank you. If you manage to think of something I've not done before, I'll accept."

He suggested nothing at all, not even the hint of an idea, for about six months. He dropped in to see her, talked about cabbages and kings and went on his way. Then, on one of his fleeting visits, he asked her casually if she had ever had tea at the Ritz on a Thursday afternoon.

"No," she said crisply. The very idea was too silly to merit more comment than that. Only tourists and ladies wearing small, expensive hats took tea at the Ritz.

"Then we shall go on Thursday," he said. "I shall pick you up at 3.30

p.m."

    He had thought of something she had never done before and she was trapped. So they sat and talked from 3.30 p.m. to 5 p.m. at the Ritz over fine bone china and dainty cakes.

    The choreography of this strange courtship changed pace but the Thin Scot danced nowhere beyond, yes, dinner and lunch.

    One day I tucked a poem into the day book, written just for her.

LET'S HAVE AN AFFAIR

But first let's make a book
with chapter, verse,
sub-section, clause,
show each impediment and cause.
Let's cite, recite,
redraft, rehearse,
decide the "ifs",
cross out the "whether",
write it on parchment,
bind it in leather,
then open it on the title page.
But let's not call it "An Affair",
with all the tangles, and the pitfalls,
with all the angles, traps and snares.
I don't want love,
you don't want marriage,
we'll shoot the horse
and burn the carriage.
There's still much to be said
for a harmless romp
in bed.
We're tall and handsome,
fun, amusing.
I scintillate,
you're stimulating.
I still resist,
you're so persistent.
Is it too late?

I'm hesitating.
Why?
Please, won't you try?
We wrote the book
with all its clauses.
We're off the hook
if we look
and don't leap
into prescribed reactions
to our prophesied actions.
If you feel a little insecure,
the cure's on page twenty-three.
If you feel like making
any unreasonable demand or two,
you'll see on page five,
all demands are taboo.

If you feel loving on Wednesday, just check and see:
the timetable's on page three.
Won't we have fun, though!
That's chapter one.
We'll see a show
page thirty-four.
We'll wine and dine
through chapter nine.
This winter we'll ski,
though next summer we'll each
lie out on a separate beach.
I'll lend you books,
you'll buy me discs,
a tie, a scarf to please.
No risks.
Some French perfume, gold pin, a pen.
You'll find a list
in chapter ten.
You'll look at me,
I'll smile at you
(that's allowed; page fifty-two).
And we'll applaud

such sophistication.
You owe me no excuse,
I'll make no explanation.
So give me your hand
and let's give it a swirl.
You see, there's no danger.
It's as safe as a bank.
And when we decide,
with panache and flair
to put an end to this affair,
then we'll ...
Oh hell, the last three pages
of our book
are blank.

It has taken her about twenty-five years to find it funny. And how did she fill those blank pages? There is no record in the Day Books and therefore not my brief to fill them in here.

I should mention that most of the gentleman callers did buy books.

Chapter 4½

Whether living my own misery or watching Ruth wade through hers, I found relief in poetry, both reading it and writing. I left the poems tucked into the Day Book and forgot about them.

Neither of us can now remember whose particular moment of pain, laughter or frustration any one poem inspired, or perhaps provoked. The writing of them helped me. Since she kept them for twenty-five years, they must have done something for her too.

NOV. 1973

All my jewelled yesterdays
have brought
such silent, brown todays.

The thought escapes me,
shimmers through my grasp
and goes,
no longer there.
Void.
There was a thought there
once before

but that escaped me too
and went.
Best to avoid another.

"WHAT NOW, MY LOVE?"

You lay by my side
and a child was born.
Lovetoken.

I lay by your side
an empty space, waiting.
Leavetaking.

You lie and by your side
I catch my breath, worn.
Heartbroken.

I lie upon my side
at my back screams distant bearbaiting.
Lovetaking.

We lie upon our backs.
Heartfaking.

R. I. PLEA

Yesterday I saw that smile
with one corner drooping down
reluctant.
Today the driver of the car in front
tilted his head to light a cigarette
and my heart went blank with joy
and my hands clasped the steering wheel
to hold me steady.
Why do my eyes
still cling to fragments of you

and try to fit them onto passers-by
when I would gladly let you go
and let me rest in peace?

THE AWAKENING

Bring back that hour
Or let me have another in its stead.
There have been hours that gleamed and shone
Linked in a chain of burnished golden days.
There have been hours like sparkling solitaires
Set in the velvet black of passing time.
But how can these compare
To that translucent hour when you, awake,
Stretched an uncertain hand towards my future
And sprinkled gold dust on my hooded lids?
The clock looks at me with its tiger's eye
And marks the hours which process in the wake
Of that elusive one you left behind.

LEARNING
I know not how to trust.
My will is bounded by my own strong arms;
What I can hold is mine.

I know not how to take.
My love I measure with a generous hand;
I have no faith in thine.

I know not how to give.
My fear of rejection turns to stone
The fingers I entwine.

There's no divinity on my horizon,
Small hope in humankind
Yet little hurt in being an island
Till now.

I know not how to live.
Tear me through these entangled barriers;
Turn water into wine.

THE NIGHT SKY IN DECEMBER

Somewhere
Beyond that galaxy
They fight the battle of the Somme
and over there
Flanders churns mud and blood.
For we have written elephantine formulae
that prove

time may be warped, twisted even
but it is unrelenting
and continues to transmit our shame
at speed beyond imagination
long after we have ceased to bang our heads.
So if you hurt me now,
The scream will travel
Through eternity.

MIRAGE IN THE RAIN

A windscreen wiper pushing at the rain
left, right, left,
a headlamp glaring in my eyes
and then your shadow
crossed my line of vision
smoky, blurred,
a needle second
and was gone.
The lights changed to green
but where was I to go
when all my will was to reverse
through raddled years

till once again I'm sitting at your side
looking at unknown, unloved faces
through a windscreen
in the rain?

AUDIT

Clerk! Put away our books,
Your careful colums neatly balanced.
One small accountant with fanatic skill
Cannot put order into merry chaos,
Computing worth and rigid circumstance.
There is no auditor.
You'll fall just as you sprung,
By chance, with not one reference
To your valour, insidious vices, half-wrought
Dreams and unfulfilled ambitions.
You claw at virtue
In fond illusion of reward,
A shred of immortality for comfort.
Your meanly hoarded credit can't discharge
The inevitable vacuum,
But move towards it quietly
And you'll learn
That in nothing there's no pain.

When troubled, Ruth kept very still and thought. She repaired books with meticulous care. She combed auction catalogues, viewed sales and was the professional bookseller. I thrashed about forgetting reason and putting it all into rhyme.

L'égarement de l'esprit par le Cœur!
L'égarement de la tête par l'esprit!
La tête ne peut être égarée que par l'esprit et l'esprit, lui alors, par beaucoup.

My head is dead.
My body shakes.
My guts are twisted.
The nights are very long.
I'm not doing very well.
If this is what quiet reflection is
All about, I'm obviously not equipped
To deal with it.

    Sometimes her logical, sensible, consistent behaviour was not easy to put up with.
    Philosophy: "Tu as souvent raison, mais c'est un tort."
    We put up with each other's "difficult" personalities in the name of Friendship.

Chapter 5

Book fairs

Incidents, anecdotes and fond memories from the many in which we exhibited over two continents and twenty-five years.

Sitting quietly at a recent book fair I overheard (loudly), "It's a nice book, but I wouldn't give him a penny over thirty thousand. Not a penny."

It was a miserable fair and times are hard, so I can't blame the man. And it was good of him to let so many of us know of his decision.

The first book fair abroad. New York.

We had been proposed, seconded and accepted as members of the Antiquarian Booksellers Association. We were in fine company and felt modestly inadequate. We were in the company of booksellers with experience and knowledge, some stretching over two or three generations; the modesty was not false. Among the many benefits the association offered, one was the right to exhibit at prestigious book fairs abroad, and within our field we felt that we now had enough books of a quality to give us the courage to do so. We filled in the forms asking for the smallest possible stand at the New York Fair and sent them off. Our application was accepted and our feet turned to ice. Should we go ahead or back out before it was too late? Ruth, as usual, paused to think. I, as usual, flapped. When in doubt, ask. So I went to Mr Maggs at Maggs Bros. a pillar of the antiquarian book world, and began to ply him with questions, questions so basic that he got the measure of our doubts and hesitation in a matter of minutes. He put spinach in my spine without being in the least condescending. Of course we had to go ahead. Why ever not?

"Choose your books, price them in dollars, make a list in triplicate and send them round here. We'll ship them with ours."

He smiled when I offered to contribute a share of the costs. When I saw their magnificent stand in New York, a few weeks later, I realised that though my offer had been polite, it would have been difficult to separate off the cost of shipping our two modest trunks.

So we chose our most beautiful children's books as our major interest and added samples of illustrated books, etiquette, schoolroom, and a few modern first editions to see what would interest the good citizens of New York. It was not only that we wanted to sell books, we wanted to broaden our American clientele. Those who had come across our stands and then our shop over the years had proved enthusiastic and loyal; we would be delighted to have more of the same.

Valentines and fragile ephemera we packed as hand luggage and landed in New York as excited as two kids. A very large porter gently took our trolley and asked us a question. There was no gainsaying him. He was a very large porter. I knew that he was asking a question because his voice rose at the end of the sentence but though I never doubted that English of a sort was spoken in America, it had never occurred to me that there was a sort that I would not be able to understand, but not a word other than "ma'am". Ruth looked at me expectantly. I was the English speaker. She smugly retired into her French nationality and waited for me to answer the porter. I asked him to repeat the question. He did. I nodded.

"What did he say?" she asked.

"Haven't a clue."

"So why did you nod?"

"Well I couldn't ask him again, could I? He looked as if he expected the answer 'yes.'"

We trotted after him as he made off on his long legs with our trolley towards the taxi rank. We had planned to take a bus into the city but as we saw our cases being stacked into a yellow cab, we followed them without protest. It would appear that the generous tip we placed into his outstretched hand was not generous enough because he stretched it out a second time. Putting the mental arithmetic of childhood to some use, we calculated that since our porter had earned ten dollars for four minutes' work and there are x-thousand passengers coming through the airport daily, and if he hijacks ten trolleys an hour it's not worthwhile becoming a brain surgeon or even a lowly bookseller.

Our hotel was not luxurious. The most scrupulous accountant and tax inspector would not have accused us of profligacy. The room was so small that one of us had to sit on her bed whilst the other took up the floor space. The fair, on the other hand, was to be held in the ballroom of one of the more renowned hotels, so we deposited our bags and walked there. We also walked back to our hotel every night during the course of the fair because we knew no better and after so many hours in the ballroom, we wanted some air, but apparently in doing so we crossed some invisible frontier which unaccompanied women do not cross at night. Perhaps it was the bliss of ignorance that kept us safe from rape and rapine or perhaps we were too weary to notice the danger lurking in the doorways.

The stands had been set up. We registered and found our modest corner where our two trunks had already been deposited by Maggs. I unpacked, Ruth organised and decorated. We worked in total silence. Our confidence was wobbly. True we had been buying and selling books for a good few years, we had an interesting list of clients and a healthy bank balance but all that was in London, England. Here we were in New York, surrounded by some of the most venerable names in the trade, who had arrived from all over the world with treasures kept in glass cases, leather binding gleaming with gilt and wax and catalogues of their stock especially printed for the occasion on that shiny, expensive paper. One or two displayed wooden escutcheons with complicated coats of arms, announcing that they supplied antiquarian books to royal and ducal houses we did not recognise but we were impressed anyway. We would have felt out of our depth were it not for the justly famed American hospitality. We were welcomed, the new kids on the block. Our children's books were admired and quite a few reserved against the opening day.

Our stand was ready. We were in New York and exhibiting at an international book fair. Why was it inappropriate to jump up and down and shout "Whoopeee!"?

We were tired, remarkably and unexpectedly relieved and decided to find something to eat. We saw the word "Deli" and walked in. The food at the counter looked good. We were shown to a table where the basket of rye bread was piled high and the bowl of salted gherkins smelled of heaven.

Our waitress walked up to us with a borderline smile. Her little brown skirt was too short, her little white lace-up boots were too tight and her hair was too gray at the roots for the brown lace and velvet coronet she bore.

"Hello ladies!" she said. "My name is Mary and I'm your waitress for this evening. Have you decided what you are going to enjoy eating with us?"

She turned expectantly to Ruth, pencil poised over pad.

"Do I have to tell her my name first?" Ruth hissed at me.

I had no more idea what were the customs of the country than she had.

"It's very nice to meet you." I said for us both.

"It's three dollars extra if you share," Mary said briskly.

Share? Why on earth would we want to share? We had not had anything to eat since the tray of imitation food presented to economy-class passengers by our airline. We were starving. So I ordered a first and second course for each of us.

"Honey," she said, "I didn't understand a word you said but I just loved the way you said it."

Ruth grunted with ill-disguised satisfaction. Not a pretty sound. The fact that I neither understood when spoken to nor managed to make myself understood with my superior Sussex boarding school English made her giggle. I just had to accept that to some on this side of the water I spoke foreign.

I jabbed the items on the menu that we wanted with a resentful finger.

"You want me to bring all that?" she asked.

"Yes please," I enunciated. "And two glasses of lemon tea."

We had not eaten in a New York deli before. When the food arrived we understood the point of the three-dollar surcharge for sharers. Never had I seen a construction of sliced meat packed between two pieces of bread so high that it had to be propped up with wooden struts to stop it keeling into the surrounding salad.

"Salt beef sandwich," said Mary, as if we could mistake it for anything else, like the Empire State Building. We hardly dared look at each other as the bowls of chopped liver, eggs and coleslaw arrived.

The next day we paid the three-dollar surcharge.

Our beautiful English accents were often admired on that and subsequent visits to the United States. Since Ruth had and continues to have a very pronounced French accent, I was annoyed and she was amused.

"But I don't sound anything like her!" said I indignantly.

"You both sound so British!"

I suppose if you go back to the Norman Conquest, we do.

"If they don't understand me," I mused just before the fair opened, "I will pass them along to you. I suppose you'd better do the same and between us we should get through."

We sold more than we would have thought possible. We met new collectors and American dealers whom we had never met before from places all over the union. There were curators from university libraries and from state and municipal libraries. I don't know if they kept a part of their budgets aside for this particular event but we were both struck by their lack of financial constraint; if a book was "needed" for their particular collection, the book was bought. Some did not even bother to ask for the discount which is traditionally offered to libraries. And our stand must have been one of the least significant in the room.

And then, after an exciting and profitable Saturday, came Sunday. We did not know that a visit to the New York book fair was a tradition for many, tucked between a lie-in and brunch. Of course those who had children brought children and what could be more interesting for these intellectual larvae than a colourful stand full of colourful old children's books? So we were plied with questions.

"Did you bring these all the way from England?"

"This is precious. Can I show it to James?"

"You mean it was really coloured by hand?"

"A hundred years old and it is still in such good condition? How was that, I wonder?"

How best to tell her that letting James have a good look at it with a sticky toffee in his hand was not going to improve the book's chance for the next hundred years?

The children were shown the illustrations, usually by parents who took care not to damage the books. But there were exceptions. Stories were read by fathers sitting cross-legged on the floor, the tabs of movable books pulled gently and less gently ... followed by heartfelt apologies but then, he's only three and doesn't know his own strength. The pile of books sold was small. The pile of books needing major and minor repairs grew apace. We asked one of our English colleagues , well known for his short fuse, how he dealt with the Sunday promenaders.

"Tell'em we're not a branch of Toys'R'Us and breakages have to be paid for."

"Oh, we couldn't do that. They would think us so rude." we said, primly.

He laughed.

"No they would not. Even those who don't know the value know the price, especially New Yorkers, and they have a healthy respect for price. Try it."

We tucked the information away for the following year, realising that it would take us about twelve months to muster that degree of bookseller's armour. Children simply had no business handling children's books but how to get that across to doting parents?

Of our two big trunks, one was going to go back to London empty and that was highly satisfactory. M. & R. Glendale were smug with satisfaction. Ruth and I in our civilian guise decided to fill the trunk. The dollar/pound exchange was in our favour and we had already noticed that in the big department stores there was a permanent sale rail in every department so we took ourselves off to Bergdorff Goodman like a hunting party, keen eyes and full wallets. After a good look round we decided to buy towels. I chose navy blue, thick velvety and heavy. Ruth went for orange. Mine were signed Missoni. Ruth's had the initials YSL prominently displayed. The price was reduced by some 60%. We looked for faults and snags and frayed edges, anything which would justify the huge reduction, but they all seemed perfect. So why should these stacks of beautiful towels be so humiliatingly reduced? Ruth turned the pile over with increasing suspicion but still could find no fault.

"Are they seconds?" I asked tentatively.

"Oh no, ma'am." the assistant replied indignantly. "They are all perfect."

"Forgive my curiosity then, but why are they all so heavily reduced?"

She waved a hand dismissively. "These? They're last season's."

I grabbed the lot. No need to tell the families back in old England that they were going to step out of the shower into last season's towels. Thirty-five years on they are still going strong but maybe they now have vintage value.

We became practised hands very quickly and exhibited in the United States twice a year, once on the East Coast and once on the West Coast in Los Angeles and San Francisco for many years. We learnt to organise the shipping, the paperwork and how to survive James's sticky fingers.

To ship your books to an overseas fair is an act of faith. You wave your pampered books good-bye, all the choosing, pricing, packing and paperwork completed and you know that when you reach your stand in New York or San Francisco, your two metal trunks will be sitting there, as if doubt were vulgar. All the same, that little tremolo of doubt is always there.

"Wouldn't it be dreadful if the books weren't waiting?" says one and the other laughs with a downward cadence and a curled lip.

There was the year when we arrived in Los Angeles and the stand was empty. The whole British contingent was in the same predicament. The truck had been delayed. We didn't know if this explanation was supposed to bring us comfort but as we looked round the group of despondent faces, no comfort was taken. The books were going to be there. We were given every assurance. They were in constant radio contact with the truck (and head office and the angel Gabriel) and they could assure us that the truck was right there on schedule. The British booksellers wandered around the hall, clockwise and anti-clockwise, looking enviously at those who had their noses in cartons with real books to unpack.

We decided that for us it was going to be hysterics or a swim. We swam. Then we had a light pool-side lunch. Then we swam again and reassured each other, of course the books would arrive and meanwhile wasn't this better than the London rain?

With three hours to go before the fair was due to open, we gazed at the pool and decided that perhaps hysterics was the more sensible option.

The books arrived and we had a good fair but our confidence was dented. When, a little while later, we decided to participate in the Amsterdam Book Fair for the first time, we also decided to pop the books in the car and take ourselves to Holland with no help from anyone. We knew that other booksellers had shipped their books but ours had been a late booking and at the time it seemed the intelligent thing to do.

We learnt all too soon that you cannot pop anywhere with a car full of books, even in friendly Europe. It's no good making intelligent suppositions when there are frontiers to be crossed. What's wanted is documents, lots of them and in many colours.

I'm the world's worst sailor. I had to leave the cinema when they were showing the Poseidon Adventure, because my stomach had turned turtle with the ship. So it was obvious that we would choose the shortest sea-crossing, even if it meant a longer drive on the other side and this involved cutting across a corner of France. This happened at the beginning of the Mitterand regime, when you were allowed to take money into France but not out of it. Since our final destination was Holland, it hadn't occurred to us that the French currency regulations might apply to us. We hadn't given them any consideration, unlike the French customs officer who stopped us at the Dutch border and he seemed seriously concerned. We were made to disgorge every pound and every centime. Every last small coin was counted. Since we were hoping to buy as well as sell, there was quite a lot to count. Ruth is French and didn't open her mouth; no excuses for her. I explained why we were in France. I pleaded. I showed them our Book Fair file. I wrung my hands. In the end, there was nothing for it and it had to be tears and sobs before we were allowed to take our money and our car full of books across the border.

This was my first trip to Amsterdam. We deposited the books on our stand, found a garage for the car and went for a walk. When we returned, a man was waiting for us. Unlike the rest of the UK contingent, our books had not been cleared by shippers. Where were our forms and how, pray, did we intend to pay our VAT? What VAT? Did we not know that there was VAT payable on our sales? On books? Certainly on books. We were ordered to pack up everything at once and take it to some shippers or to a customs house. He pointed a finger at the exit. We sat determinedly on our boxes. What would he need? Surely if we brought a list of books and their values, there was no need to bring the books themselves. Could he not vouch for the fact that the boxes contained books and not bullion or cocaine? He looked doubtful. I gave Ruth a look that told her that if tears had to be brought out again, it was her turn.

Well, yes, if one of us were to go with him, matters could be put right. Forms would have to be filled in. A shipper employed. The length and breadth of Amsterdam covered so that the pink copy of the blue form should lie snugly in the yellow folder. A deposit to the value of the VAT payable if we sold every single book we had brought would have to be paid. The difference would be returned to us against invoices at the end of the fair.

I did a rapid calculation and swallowed hard. Then I smiled at the official, my partner and the world in general. I had taken precautions! I had armed myself with a gold credit card so that just such a problem would immediately cease to be one. Their publicity booklet had told me so.

Both the shippers and the customs' officials behaved as if a case such as ours had never been known before. They chewed the dens of the pencils, tapped their computers and waited for salvation from their superior's superior. Was there, perhaps, a patron saint of Customs and Excise who would give ultimate guidance? I was taken from office to office, each with interior décor inspired by Orwell. I was treated fairly. There were no questionable interrogation tactics. We were in a civilised country but I was made to feel that I was guilty of dark, nameless crimes. I was causing disruption and disturbing the immaculate order of a working day. Glendale, with its carload of undocumented books, had brought the menace of chaos to the Dutch Republic.

A hefty four-figure sum would be needed before we would be allowed to sell a single book. I nodded nonchalantly and took a taxi to Barclay's Bank, an imposing building on the smartest of the canals.

The elderly Schwarzenegger at the door asked me my business. His square head was imperfectly covered by a round, peaked cap. Gold buttons strained across his chest.

"Oh," I said, with all the confidence of one freshly armed with gold plastic. "I need to pick up some money."

"Well, you can't pick it here."

His English was not faultless but determined.

"According to my handbook, I can."

I waved the handbook at him, the rich brown and gold of the covers emphasising my superior status. "I can draw up to £7,000, use your telex, and call on your help in every way."

"Not here. This is not a bank for people."

"No? What's it for then?"

"Business. We do business with companies, not people."

"There's no other branch in Amsterdam, so can I speak to somebody here?"

"No, my job not permit you to go there."

He pointed to the shrines behind him. They looked like ordinary offices to me. I argued. I realised that a platinum card studded with diamonds would not move him, let alone my poor ersatz gold.

The president of the Dutch ABA bailed us out, paid the VAT, took responsability for our good behaviour, completed all the formalities, signed forms in many colours and took us back to the fair in his car.

Still bruised, I spent the quiet moments of the fair composing suitable letters to Barclay's.

At the end of the fair we paid our VAT, retrieved the balance of our deposit and left for Zeebrugge, avoiding France and obeying every instruction to the letter. We registered our departure from Holland, leaving a copy of the pink form at the customs office and registered our arrival in England, leaving a copy of the blue form and the green form with Sheerness customs, who would send them on to Holland.

Two months later we received a menacing letter to the effect that since the blue form and green form had not arrived in Amsterdam to join the pink form, we had obviously sold all our books somewhere between Amsterdam and Zeebrugge, so would we please remit that balance of the deposit of the VAT that had been returned to us. We replied briefly. The second letter was more menacing. The third letter threatened fire and brimstone. It took two years to unravel the knot and we never did receive an acknowledgement of our spotless innocence. We never exhibited in Amsterdam again. We were cured of DIY transport to Book Fairs and intelligent guesswork. We handed our books over to shipping agents with gratitude and an infantile faith that nanny would get it right for us.

The one delightful memory that remains of that particular bookfair is of the elderly gentleman, whose shoes shone, detachable white collar with tie knotted high up his throat, and tweed jacket respectable with age, who sat next to our stand for most of each day. He spoke the perfect English of a different era, the English his nanny had taught him. Every evening, just before he left, he rose and with a slight bow, apologised,

"Forgive me ladies, that I must now be on my way. Good night and toodle pip!"

We wondered if he had his Spitfire parked outside.

Keep overheads down. Money is to be spent on books and not on trimmings. Think before you order a dozen dozen.

We didn't embroider cross-stitch samplers of the house rules but they were deeply etched on the mind. We dismissed expensive note-paper with matching envelopes, carrier bags and printed invoice books as trimmings. Stamps were second class. Coffee came with digestive biscuits. In the best war-time tradition, what could be salvaged and re-used was neatly folded and put away. We vied with each other in outbursts of frugality.

When the information pack came for the Maastricht Book Fair we sniffed disparagingly at the favourable rates offered to the participants by the local hotels. Much too extravagant for us, we decided. A simple pension was good enough. We found a list in an old Michelin and with a street plan of the town in front of us we rang a few in the vicinity of the exhibition hall stipulating only that we needed twin beds and an en suite bathroom. We chose one that sounded most reasonable and which mein host described in glowing terms in excellent English. We would have many beds, yes, a bathroom, yes, and the best coffee in the whole of Holland. It seemed too good to miss.

We climbed the steep stairs and opened the door hesitantly. Somehow the hotel was a little more scruffy than our worst fears. Dim light bulbs obscured multitudes of sins for only a few seconds before the eye focused on the stained wallpaper Intermezzo, then looked away from the greasy bald patches on the banquettes in the reception area. The linoleum on the stairs was the same pattern as the one used everywhere in my old boarding school, and that brought a rush of memories prompted more by dry rock buns than Mr Proust's delicate cakes. In the room there were many beds, yes. There were five, to be exact, narrow and covered with thin, monastic blankets. In one corner, on a podium, was a bath, a basin and a lavatory, separated from the main body of the room by an opaque glass screen some three feet high on which you could rest your chin and thus sit and discuss philosophy with your friends. Neither partnership nor friendship could put up with that degree of Roman intimacy.

There was a single bulb shining bleakly at the end of its flex, swinging gently in the draught, yet the room was overheated and the windows did not open. We asked if we might have a room with fewer beds, perhaps (it had crossed our minds that three more people might be coming to join us but then dismissed the idea as ludicrous) and a more secluded bathroom. Mein host chose to look blank. We had asked for an en suite bathroom, hadn't we? Well, this was better than en suite, it was au beau milieu! He guffawed triumphantly at his own mastery of international wit. So what were we whining about? Chastened we returned to our room and planned a tolerable way of life for the next few days, which involved a certain amount of time spent in the cold corridor for each of us in turn.

That book fair was very successful so that we could admit that frugality had crossed the border into downright stinginess. Running a small business effectively did not include mortification of the flesh. We made up for the spartan accommodation by dining very well indeed.

Having chosen the name for our enterprise, now officially a registered partnership, we opened a bank account, bought a ledger to keep the account straight, stamps, envelopes, the necessary equipment for packing good, strong parcels and the first Day Book. It was intended, with almost pompous seriousness to be a log for orders, requests, enquiries and all sorts of professional matters. It didn't take long for all sorts of unprofessional matters to creep in, sometimes heavily underlined.

"You left the light on AGAIN."

"Is that an order of Aladdin or Al Din or All In?? For heaven's sake, do something about your writing!"

"Can I borrow your big le Creuset for Saturday. I want to make a cassoulet."

"Don't wear that hat. It makes you look like a pudding." (That's friendship for you at the end of a working day.)

We even had a heated row over several tightly scrawled pages, without having the least glimmer, thirty-five years down the road, what sparked off the storm. It makes trawling through our Glendale years more fun than yet another memo noting yet another order for a pristine limited edition of the unattainable at a price that was risible even then.

Then there was the name. Having decided on Glendale, we quickly became secretive about its origin. Perhaps we felt that the way we had put it together was a little childish. We didn't want to be told a second time that it was "sweet" or be asked if we were going to change it should one of us move to Offord Street, for instance. We could be Glenford or Offdale! The permutations for inventing double meanings of various shades of blue appeared to be endless. We could not fathom why this word game should reduce our colleagues to helpless mirth, so whenever we were asked, we opted for tight lipped mystery.

Then we discovered that there was a place called Glendale in California and passing Californians greeted us warmly and asked us whereabouts in Glendale we had our shop and were amazed that they had never come across us there but had to come all the way to London, England to trip over our charming stock. It was hard to explain that the name was born of two streets in London NW3 and impolite to own up that our knowledge of geography did not stretch to Glendale, Ca.

We became defensive. After the successful fair in Maastricht our welcoming Dutch colleagues organised a dinner. There was a lot of wine on the table. Ruth and I were the only young women in partnership to have exhibited. It was assumed, taken for granted even, that our partnership extended well beyond our interest in books. Slowly, the attention of several people at our table focused on the two of us and the most tactful key to the nature of our relationship seemed to be in the origin of Glendale. It became an after dinner game. It attracted more people.

"Is it a family name?"

"No."

"But is there anybody in the family called Glendale?"

"No."

"Well, Glen at least?"

"No."

"You took it from the telephone book with a pin!"

"We wouldn't use a pin. Dangerous things, pins."

"Without a pin then, just at random."

Ruth hesitated, looking pensive.

"There's a place in California called Glendale, near Los Angeles," she offered.

"Is that where you come from?" someone jumped in triumphantly.

She looked blank.

"No," she said, as if she could not see what connection there could be between what she had just said and the question that followed.

"But has it got anything to do with California?"

"No."

So that particular seam of possibilities was exhausted.

"It must come from somewhere." someone suggested vaguely.

"Yes."

"So? Is it a code? You know, like a Masonic handshake that you have to be in the loop to recognise."

"Loop?" Ruth's talent for putting a crescendo on the French accent and at the same time looking innocently blank was worthy of a serious acting accolade. She was perfectly capable of pronouncing "loop" without stretching the word through three syllables and covering half a major scale.

The effort to enlighten her came from one of our team of British exhibitors.

"You know, is it a name that would be recognised by someone belonging to an organisation but wouldn't mean anything to anyone outside it?"

Ruth now chose to look profoundly intelligent, her brow furrowed with comprehension.

"Like IBM?"

"IBM?"

"Yes," she explained, "that's a very large organisation."

"No," our English colleague sighed, "that's not exactly what I had in mind. I'm sure you didn't get Glendale from IBM. No, I meant a sort of fraternity, a combined interest in something, a complicity."

The glint in Ruth's eye was difficult to interpret. She was either going to move smoothly on to stamp collecting or even more smoothly to happy lesbian organisations whose members communicated their affiliation by whispering "Glendale" as they slipped through the door.

"It's really very simple," I cut in. If Ruth chose to be the dumb brunette with baby blue eyes for the evening, I was going to have to play the sharp and witty redhead. (My choice of hair colour in those days was a moveable feast.)

"It's really very simple." I repeated. "We made the name up from important bits of our lives. "G" was the initial of Ruth's first lover and "Len" was the name of mine but by happy coincidence "LE" were also the initials of her fifth who was terribly important for a while, so we managed to cover a lot there very neatly. Then "D" was my fourth and "Al" was her first husband and "E" is the initial of my present incumbent so that makes up Glendale. The "M" and "R" at the beginning stand for Monika and Ruth."

Ruth nodded her agreement, serious as a pope. I looked around as if I had solved the mystery of the square of the hypotenuse in three easy steps with a little QED at the end, as is only proper.

Our English brigade looked away embarrassed but I would never have expected our Dutch hosts to greet our explanation with such stuffy disapproval. There were several weighty seconds of silence and then everyone began to talk at once about all sorts of fascinating things, but not, I think, about any kind of lovers or acronyms.

Intermezzo

It wasn't all books. There were homes, husbands, the toll of sons rose to five as I gambled for a daughter and produced a third son. There were shopping expeditions. There were concerts and plays and all the good things London has to offer. There were inevitable dinner parties, the competetive entertainment of the comfortable young married couples nesting in North London (avocado, prawns and three desserts!). The accumulation of wedding presents gleamed on starched tableclothes. As the years passed, the tablecloths disappeared, the tables got scratched and dinner parties relaxed into shared meals with friends. The wedding china gave way to pottery, sturdy and replaceable. There was a lot of laughter. The boys got on well until, at about the age of 15, one of mine decided he couldn't stand one of hers. There wasn't much in the world he could stand, a particularly difficult adolescent who emerged from his prickly chrysalis as a particularly delightful man. But oh, the time it took!

Before the wars of adolescence broke out we shared our summer holidays. According to Ruth's French tradition, city children may be fatally impaired if they do not breathe sea air for one month in the summer, the month being July or August. So every year we rented a house in France or Spain or Portugal and packed a month's supply of necessities, our bouquet of boys and set off to breathe sea air. Husbands came for the last two weeks. The husbands got on well enough. They did not have much in common and never became friends but tolerated each other in a bluff, back-slapping way. It sufficed. Later in our lives, after the two marriages broke up, they did not see each other.

The first year we decided on Le Touquet and chose to look for the house ourselves rather than rely on carefully angled photographs that conceal the six-lane motorway running through the front garden or the estate agent's hysterical superlatives. We would inspect our summer residence ourselves.

In those far-off days, there were flights from Kent to Le Touquet in small planes that held two cars and a few passengers sitting, as if on safari, on canvas seats. The flight took twenty minutes. Ruth's parents had driven up from Paris and were there to greet us. So we had lunch overlooking the wide golden sands of Le Touquet, glowing in bright sunshine. We lingered. Then we ambled down the main shopping street, drooling over silk scarves and crocodile handbags. Ruth's mother remarked that the sun was somewhat low in the sky. It was four o'clock and we hadn't spotted a single agency. We hadn't even remembered to look for one.

We needed a house with three or four bedrooms, one large enough for all the boys to share, as near to the sea as possible, with the usual offices. We were delighted with the very first house on offer. Beginner's luck! We paid our deposit and left for the airstrip. Ruth's mother handed us a packet of sandwiches she had prepared at dawn in Paris, carefully wrapped, in case one of us should feel faint for lack of nourishment on the twenty-minute flight back to Kent and we all waved frantic handkerchieves as the plane buzzed away.

It was "the usual offices" that was the problem when we arrived on the first day of our holiday. When we had inspected the house we had noted with satisfaction that there were two bathrooms, one for the adults and one for the children we had decided. What we had not noted, and to this day I lay the blame entirely at Ruth's door, is that French bathrooms, especially in older buildings, do not come complete with lavatory. That unpleasant necessity is kept separate, in a corner usually windowless and badly lit. In this house, the one and only lavatory was under the stairs on the ground floor, with no hand basin and lit with a 25-watt bulb. Just the one for five adults (two husbands to come and one young lady au pair to help with the children, and she from a good Swiss home with a superior sense of comfort and hygiene). The husbands, when they arrived, refused to believe that the lavatories we were so sure we had seen in the bathrooms in May had been whisked away by malicious fairy plumbers by August.

On that first holiday it rained solidly, miserably for the first three days and we sat with our four small children, a tight-lipped au pair and two bathrooms, one lavatory. The sun did eventually come out and we learnt to form an orderly queue.

After that we chose with somewhat greater care. In Spain we taught the boys to play poker. We played five-card stud, then seven, cards open, closed, adders, leaners and every improbable variation unknown to the pros in Las Vegas. Ruth's No. 2 son, not exactly dim (an exhibition to Cambridge came some years later, a seemly recompense for not grasping the principles of poker in nursery school), was slow on the uptake, so Ruth decided on a little extra coaching.

I came out of the shower, my head wrapped in a towel, to see small son, huge brown eyes brimming, and mother, huge blue eyes smouldering, shouting across the table, "How many times do I have to tell you that fours beats full house?"

Very gently, so as not to upset her further, I hinted that perhaps when he had lost his milk teeth he might get the hang of it.

We look through our photo albums and giggle over "Do you remember?" There was the inevitable rush of grilled sardines in Portugal, delicious the first day but looking too much like dead fish by the end of the second week. There was the boys' battle with shaving foam. There was the house with the huge fig tree in the garden where we picked the figs for breakfast every morning. There was the year the boys learnt to swim, had a go at riding without great success, to play volleyball and the guitar. Ruth and I went to the market, swam, sat in the sun and watched them grow. And we talked. We never stopped talking and still haven't.

Just a few years ago we took four grandchildren to the seaside in England, this time three boys and one dainty girl (hers, not mine), and as we fussed over bruised knees and read stories perched on their beds, we felt we had wound back the tape. It was only the odd glance in the mirror that prodded us back to the reality of the years that had passed, endlessly astonished how the outer shell ages so much more quickly than the core.

We have no memory of rows on holiday or at home. Browsing through the Day Books, however, we came across some really meaty ones that lasted for several weeks. What were they all about? We admire the level of invective, the flow of the logic, the scrupulously neat handwriting as the anger mounted, lest swirls and splodges betray bad temper. Yet there is no clue as to what sparked them off. It could not have been over blunders, a mispriced book or a careless collation, because the deal was that when that happened, one would dig the other one out of the hole and not bury her in it. That was plain common sense. I think that we came out even in the blunders department over the years. It's almost sad not to be able to remember what so much hot ink was about.

PARENTS' DAY

With five sons, we ran into the usual measles in those pre-jab days, chicken pox and whoop, the troubles and triumphs of school, sibling punch-ups naturally; we were the poor parents who often felt that we didn't understand anything.

Ruth, who had gone to school in France, sometimes felt mauled by the English system where the unwritten constitution based on tradition had to be absorbed rather than learnt, so I wrote this to make her smile in the mid-1970s. She does not have a son called Henry!

I am a Parent
and I come in huge white shoes
with my head poked forward
to balance the borrowed hat,
bearing the loops of handbag over my left arm.
You stand by your raised desk
in your comprehensive kingdom
divinity for the last Saturday of the term
(but morning only)
surveying knots of anxious parents
trying to catch your eye
and to avoid it.

"Ah, young Henry's mother!"
and I simper into my identity.
My dress has too many flowers
and orange blobs
and it pulls across the bottom where I have grown
since last year.
Lord, no wonder Henry has problems you
say, but you only say,
"Aggressive little chap, isn't he?" and you laugh because of
course you have it all under control
in spite of me.

"He discharges it all on the younger, weaker boys
at the moment
but when we have taught him
to channel it into more positive
channels, ha, ha,
you know
who knows
what great things …?"

A bully.
"He's very nice at home
and always helps with the washing-up."
"They always are." You dismiss Henry's evening piles
of pots and plates
with a professional smile, experience, knowledge,
three books on child psychology,
and plunge him in the cesspool
with the "they".

And the little knot lower their voices,
strain their ears,
so that's his mother,
poor cow,
should take a strap to him
gave my poor Clive a black eye,
too sensitive to give him one back, of course.
Of course.

Oh great white chief in your Sunday suit
if I were to meet you in the long queue at Sainsbury's
in your shabby Friday trousers
and me in my jeans
we could chat about the price of beef
and PAYE
and Henry,
bull-necked
hard-eyed
Henry, with calloused fists.
Mine.
Here, in my borrowed uniform
of Parent on Parade
Henry is yours, and my slap-dash, slovenly
homework
makes it difficult for you to make progress
so I mumble about my broken pencils,
lost pen
and, contrite, promise to do better next term.

But just you wait, young Henry
till I get home.
I'll teach you a thing or two.

My No. 3 son, the one who was supposed to have been a girl but wasn't, one morning had had enough.
"You must get up."
"You must clean your teeth."
"You can't possibly go to school in those muddy shoes."
"You must not slide down the banisters like that."
So he stood in front of this bullying robot that was his mother, drew himself up to his full three feet and six inches and yelled:
"I don't want to have to must!"
I wrote this for him in the shop as an apology.

I don't want to have to must
put on the other sock
now,
brush my teeth when
I like the taste of yellow,
brush my hair to kill
the night-friendly hedgehog,
brush my shoes to lose
all that wealthy mud
and high time
learn to tell the time
so that it can ever after
tell me.

I don't want to have to must.
I'd rather make aeroplane noises
loud
and bank down the stairs,
strife the cornflakes
and the cat
late, well anyway
long after eight.

I don't want to have to must.
I'd rather lie on the floor,
sprawl
until I've thought of six things
I mustn't.

A PROPHECY

I am going to be a dreadful old woman.
I am. I mean, look,
the choice is so narrow.
Either I'll cut my hair short
and stride
or I'll dye it pale sky
and weave wafer hands
around gracious opinions.
I'll remember and remember gauze summers
and everlasting teas on sunlit lawns
in Hampshire.
I can gather artistic flow
and heave a long bosom swathed in natural calico
over the cobalt of the new brush
emerged triumphant from his one-man show,
his first, held in
the foyer of Upminster Public Library.
Then I can go for politics, local
or good works, parochial
and wear a hat.
I can mount a camel
and beneath the banner of my liberation rampant
on leathered skin
scythe through reluctant harems in Arabia.
I'm told they still abound.
Or there's chronic hypochondria
and merry rounds round Harley Street
and my appointment at the hospital
department of bunions

but such an interesting case, he said,
I feel quite proud.
I can cook spiced delicacies
and let my thighs grow
and my supplement smile.
Or I can grow my mind
rooting in musty manuscripts and learned papers
and publish.
Or I can prey on my children
and pray to them.
I brought them up, they owe me
so please won't you let me baby sit
and let me be grateful but make sure
that you are too.
Or maybe I'll just die.
It's dramatic but it is quick.

I slipped this into the Day Book. I have always found birthdays heavy going but every year seem to recover nicely by February 16th.
"Here is another one for your collection.
The result of a dark brown week-end where the futility of every movement struck me as quite obvious. The mood passes, little damage is done, and we continue to make movements, futile or otherwise.
Tomorrow is my thirty-ninth birthday."

Ruth did not bother to reply to either the poem or the gloomy little note that came with it but some thirty years later, she sent me back my poem, which I had long forgotten, and asked me how good a prophet did I think I had been. I replied.

So here we are,
Two old women,
Dreadful perhaps each in her way.
We knew the choice would be narrow
But we edged through
Day by day by night.
The hair is grey.
Hers more, mine less.

The waist is not an isthmus
Any more,
A solid land mass
Between boob and hip.
Hers less, mine more.
We neither jump as high
Nor run as long
But yet we glide, a little slow,
Evading sunlit lawns,
Those one-man shows,
Proud bunions, harems,
Politics, local. Good works, parochial
And musty manuscripts.
We neither pray nor prey
On sons full grown
With children of their own.
We knit them little sweaters,
Teach them their letters
And spin them stories
About old magic days
When webs were spun
Not clicked.
We've time to stand and stare
At star and cloud,
To air rigid opinions
At any wedding guest
Who comes our way.

If old's a destination
Then we are here.
Dreaded, not dreadful yet.
Give it another year.
Aged 67 1/2.

Chapter 6

Keeping the shop stocked

The main problem with running an antiquarian bookshop, or even a modest book room, is that you can't ring up the publisher and ask for another dozen. So with the pleasure of selling a book, especially a thick one, comes the slightly sinking feeling at the sight of the three-inch gap left on the shelf. Customers tend to come by regularly, often with that apologetic question "Anything new for me?" And they would rather see something that isn't quite right, just out of their field, than not be offered anything that they haven't already seen last week. So the chase for new stock is relentless.

The round of auctions in London was a necessary chore. The competition for the best items was stiff and for a good few years we were in no position to bid against the representatives of the old established firms sitting confidently in the chairs assigned to them by custom. We chewed our pencils and hoped that the odd crumb would come our way. The only thing to do was to take in as many country auctions as we could, as far from London as possible, and if the book section of the catalogue read as if had been put together by the auctioneer's most junior assistant, so much the better. There could be hidden treasures, first editions, association copies, an autographed letter from Elizabeth I or Newton tucked carelessly between two pages. As we struggled out of our beds on black winter mornings, it was that combination of hope and imagination that kept us going.

The sales started at 11.00 a.m. sharp. The viewing started at 9.30 a.m., sometimes not quite so sharp. If we tore the catalogue down the middle, we could squeeze in exactly three woman hours of viewing. But before that we had to get ourselves to Exeter or Bristol, Bath or Brighton without breaking the speed limit. The book auctions almost always took place the day before the sale of Furniture and Misc., so the first thing to do was to spot the two most comfortable armchairs among the next day's lots and mark them as ours by loading them with newspapers, our warm hats, anything would do, like the loathsome tourists who spread out their towels on the best loungers by the hotel pool before going in to breakfast. Then we could turn our attention to the shelves of books, the tables spread with pamphlets and prints and the boxes of job lots.

At eleven o'clock we sank into our armchairs and compared notes, decided how much we were prepared to bid on any one lot and marked the potential sleepers that almost inevitably someone else had spotted as well: that letter from Elizabeth I never did turn up. We bought a coffee and a sandwich. The lots we wanted were almost always in huddles of five or six with stretches of military history to sit through patiently in between. A good auctioneer could get through as many as a hundred lots an hour but even so, there was all too often an hour or even an hour and a half with nothing for us and the voice at the end of the room droning gently on and on. One would read the paper and do the crossword with half an ear open. The other one dozed. This was when that lift of excitement that had got us through some three hours of driving and an hour or two of intense viewing began to ebb. Country auctions are often held in halls, barns, old hangars divided by flimsy partitions into more manageable spaces but with any heating available blowing exclusively at the auctioneer's feet. No amount of fur boots and layers of husbands' socks seemed able to keep the feet at human blood temperature. The miscellany of items prepared for the next day's sale, faded chintz on weary chairs, unwanted vases, the detritus of others' lives, began to close in. The greenish woman in the portrait hanging askew was staring at us with a malicious eye. It is all too easy to slip into melancholy when you are tired, cold and getting colder and the next lot marked in your catalogue is not coming up for hours. Inevitably there were days when the one on duty, deputed to stay alert, dozed too, but only very lightly so that when the number registered somewhere at the back of sleep was called out, the eyes sprang open and the hand sprang up.

"Lot two-hundred and twenty-five. What am I bid?" can sound just like "Lot three-hundred and twenty-five. What am I bid?"

Lots can only be paid for and collected at the end of the sale, so one of us would queue to pay and the other for the attention of the porter, the only one allowed to distribute lots against a signed receipt. Then came the loading of the books into the car and the long drive home, giggling triumphantly or with just two small lots in an oversized box rattling on the back seat and a box of military history, unloved, unwanted but reluctantly paid for, lot two hundred and twenty five.

Whilst we were selling from Barrett Street and later from Gray's, we were rarely offered books, let alone whole collections. Once in the shop however, the offers came in often. Sometimes a single book was put on the table for our inspection. Sometimes it seemed to rain books, especially when the weather was warm and we left the door of the shop open. That was the season of unsolicited books.

The first was dropped without ceremony in the middle of the floor.
"Hold on a minute, I've got three more in the taxi."
Three more would duly arrive.
"I saw your shop when we were driving past last night. I'm sure you'll like these but I can't stop now. Taxi's waiting. I'll give you a call later!"
And there we were, left with four huge boxes of books where they blocked the entrance and caused bruising. Barbara Cartland and Reader's Digest shrunken classics have their place in the firmament but not in ours. Why did we let them do it? Natural curiosity, I suppose. We could never resist a box of books, unsorted, uncharted, sure to contain an undiscovered page of Caxton, an undocumented first edition of Alice in Wonderland, a letter from George Washington slipped in as a bookmark, in which he ponders on the nature of Truth and fruit trees. Over the years the nuggets were small and infrequent but the excitement was always there. At worst, we sometimes came across a book we had wanted to read for years.

Like the first cuckoo, the first consignment of the season would arrive. There was one particularly surly couple who arrived with three boxes of books and then stood silently hand in hand in the doorway. I patted the boxes by way of welcome. When they left, I started sorting at once, just to clear the clutter.

The books had a very definite theme. There must have been every book on selling and on management skills written in the last ten years. There were books on improving your self-image and improving your technique at interviews. There were books on how to sell yourself at interviews and how to manage your self-image. There were heavy hardbacks from America and scrawny pamphlets promising instant success.

Were I to buy them, we would have to open a new section in the basement. Were I not to buy them, it would mean that after such profound study and research, my surly young couple would have to admit that they could not sell three boxes of second-hand books to a second-hand bookseller. It seemed an unkind cut.

Within a day, the pair were back, hand in hand. "How much did you have in mind?" I asked tentatively.

"We don't care. We're emigrating on Thursday."

I wondered if this was the best of sales techniques. Perhaps something had escaped them in their reading. Or perhaps my thoughts on the subject were old-fashioned and this was the New Wave Selling Method.

I named a price.

"Cash," she said, putting out her hand.

So suddenly we had two shelves of books, very modestly priced where the philosopher's stone may yet be lurking.

The nuggets were few but they did come to find us.

"It's not exactly a book, but I thought you might like this," said the very elderly lady and from her bag pulled out a rectangular box. And there was Phoebe, a small paper doll in her bloomers, with a full wardrobe of hand-coloured dresses, coats and hats and at her side a tiny wooden cheval mirror, its silver crackled with age, all in pristine condition. I had seen pictures of Phoebe in catalogues but never held her in my hand before. She was exquisite, each paper garment complete with its dainty tabs to be folded over her shoulders. Nothing was missing.

"I would like to buy her," I said. "How much did you have in mind?"

All the gamesmanship, the assumed lack of interest, the little moue of reluctance went by the board.

"She's exquisite," I sighed.

The old lady glowed with pleasure and named a price that would have made the head buyer at Asprey blanch, had Asprey dealt in such treasures.

This was no fairy godmother in disguise.

"I am sorry," I said, putting Phoebe back in her box. "I would love to buy her but that is much, much more than I can afford."

She slipped Phoebe in her box back into her bag with satisfaction.

"I never really wanted to sell her anyway," she said, "but when I do, I'll sell her to you."

"Why?"

"Because you said you couldn't afford her. You didn't tell me she wasn't worth it. My little Phoebe is worth every penny."

A couple of months later she came in and sold Phoebe to Ruth for a very reasonable price. We kept her for a long time, exhibiting her eventually at an international fair with a perfectly silly price tag, hoping thus to keep her a little longer, but she was snapped up within half an hour of the fair opening.

There is no shortage of old ladies in Marylebone.

I remember another one who charmed her way into the shop. She wanted to chat.

"Oh, I do love to talk to young people!" she said, looking at me. Well, I suppose to somebody of ninety-two, I qualified.

"I can't stand people of my own age." she said vehemently. "They're either potty or they talk about their pains. Who wants to listen to a catalogue of operations?"

She mentioned, quite casually, that she had some books to sell. We agreed that I would come to see her the following Sunday. She lived in a mansion block near the shop, where there is a new predatory breed of traffic warden, the kind that gives the meter a little kick to help the "excess charge" click into place promptly. Sunday is a good day to view books in central London and I duly arrived at 3 p.m., dressed for work and probably dusty work at that. The door was opened by Mrs P., wearing a little black velvet number, pearls, antique diamond pin, patent pumps, with her hair freshly curled round her face and tinted a delicate blue. Behind her stood a genuinely young man, with eyes rounded like a startled bush baby.

And behind him was a table festively laid for tea, with silver tea-pot, rich fruit cake and damask napkins folded next to white china plates. This was not to be a quick cup of tea to moisten a dry throat coated with book dust.

"Two of you! Do come in. I can't tell you how long it is since I had two people here at the same time."

She introduced me to her great-nephew (or was it great-great?) who lived in Scotland and was passing through on his way to Rome. He was going to stay the night in her spare room and catch a plane the following morning. He had wanted to take her out but she didn't go to the theatre any more and she didn't eat enough to justify going to a restaurant but two people for tea was as good as a party. Her great-nephew was delighted to help and was waiting with enormous interest to meet me. She had told him all about our shop, an oasis of civilisation in Thatcherite Marylebone. Would I please tell them more about it? Would I tell them about how we had started out? Would I tell them all about books? Her great-nephew was so interested in old books! She patted a comfortable chair and I sat down.

The nephew nodded dumbly as his great-aunt vaunted his enthusiasm. He looked as if he were suffering third-degree boredom and I had yet to open my mouth. Whatever my plans may have been for the rest of the afternoon, I put a line through them. I could not be sure if there were, in fact, any books for me to look at and it would have been churlish to ask. What was certain was that I had been hijacked to a tea-party, and there was nothing to do but enjoy it.

The nephew asked a polite question or two. I accepted a cup of tea and a neat triangle of bread. I launched in on the history of books, starting with papyrus, the Great Library of Alexandria, via Books of Hours, William Caxton, all the way to Penguin. I thought I had done well in twenty minutes. I felt a kinship with Sheherezade. The nephew was catatonic. Mrs P. was rosy with pleasure.

"Oh, do tell us some more!" she goaded.

I looked at the nephew and smiled.

"Perhaps another time."

His relief was palpable.

"Wouldn't you like to see the books my aunt wants to sell?" he said, all but levitating from his chair in his eagerness to change the subject.

So there were books to be seen. I had almost forgotten about them.

"Do come along," said Mrs P. and led me along a dark corridor to an unused, half-furnished dining room. There was a huge chandelier in a tea-chest in the middle of the room. The furniture that was still there was very beautiful, including one bookcase full of books. She looked around her and waved an arm towards the furniture.

"I never had any children, you know, so I haven't anybody to leave this to. I did give a few bits to my sister's family but they don't seem at all interested in this old stuff. Come to think of it, I can't stand the sight of it any more myself. Some of it was my mother's, so I've been looking at it all my life, and that's far too long. Now, when I want some fun, I sell a piece."

"You mean you sell one piece at a time?" I asked.

"Yes," she giggled. "I choose an antique dealer and invite him up to buy one piece. They all seem to want to buy everything. I don't know why they get so cross with me, but their offers do go up in the most ridiculous way, as if I were an auction. But then, I don't need the money and it's so much fun watching them getting all steamed up. They think I've lost my marbles, the way they talk to me."

I wondered if this was a warning shot across my bows. The nephew hovered protectively just inside the door, as if I were about to bludgeon his frail relative for her paperbacks.

"Does that mean you only want to sell one book at a time?"

She burst into peals of laughter.

"What a wonderful idea! I hadn't thought of it, but a wonderful idea!"

I sat back on my heels and waited. She stopped laughing and pondered.

"No, I don't suppose that would really work. You'd better have them all."

Whilst I looked through the books, the nephew stood unblinking in the doorway. He had much to teach the dummies at Madame Tussauds. There were some three hundred books, good basement stock, the books of someone who bought at random, with no more than a superficial interest in any one subject. There were three books on chess, a few good novels, a well-bound set of some author long forgotten, a few biographies, half a dozen histories of London and a similar quantity on fishing. There was no early Auden or Ezra Pound, no signed copies, nothing to lift the heart. The period was correct but the interest had not been there. I made an offer somewhat tinged by my disappointment. Mrs P. was delighted.

"What a lot of money! How simply splendid! I shall go out tomorrow and buy a silk frock. Oh, I shall enjoy myself!"

She busied herself piling the books into bags and boxes, afraid that her nephew would be too slow and that I might change my mind.

The nephew helped me carry the books downstairs and load the car.

"What are you going to do with them now?" he asked.

"With what?"

"The books."

"How do you mean?"

"Well, where are you going to take them?"

"To my shop. Your aunt told you we have a shop near here."

"And you're going to sell them?"

He shook his head. His eyes had the unfortunate tendency to look completely round when he lifted his eyebrows, like shiny brown marbles stuck into a snowman's face.

"I hope so, eventually. What did you think I was going to do with them?"

His attitude made me cross. How could he possibly dismiss a whole boot full of good reading?

"I don't know. I thought you must have been sent by some agency or other."

He waved a disparaging hand over the boxes, now carefully arranged in the boot of the car.

"I'm not quite sure what you imagine," I said tartly, slamming the lid shut. "Do you think I've come from some agency for distressed gentlefolk that hands out money with great tact, by pretending to buy their possessions?"

"Something like that."

"But your aunt is not distressed."

"She's over ninety and living by herself. All her friends are dead. That's distressing enough, isn't it?"

"Yes, but buying her old books isn't going to relieve that very much, is it?"

He didn't reply and walked away.

Going to look at books in people's homes does expose you to the strangest attitudes but here was a possibility of offering kindness by stealth that had probably never occurred to any charitable organisation on the register.

A few days later Mrs P. was back in the shop, in great form. In her bag she had two books that she put on the desk. They were old reference books on lace and I duly admired them. She looked a little sheepish.

"Would you like to come to tea on Sunday?" she asked. "We can have scones and fruit cake and you can look at the books in my husband's study. I think you'll like them."

Sometimes the invitation to buy a collection of books took an unexpected turn.

The son-in-law was a pleasant young man, dark suit, polished shoes and the sort of striped tie that may have been regiment or old school for those who can decipher these things. We had seen him in the shop quite often, obviously during his lunch hour, when he browsed and bought inexpensive books from our basement, books for reading rather than collecting. After paying, he always stayed at the desk to talk for a few minutes about nothing in particular, with the usual charm that these little exchanges demand.

One day, he stopped for a few extra minutes, uncomfortably hesitant, as if waiting to be helped out of a hole.

"Yes?"

"My father-in-law died quite recently," he blurted out. This was news removed from the bland chats about the chill of summer and the catastrophe of the cricket score.

"I am sorry to hear that."

"Yes. Thank you. He was quite old really," he said, as if to forestall the least hint of an untimely exit. "Nearly ninety. He married very late. My wife is his only child and she and her mother want to sell the house as quickly as possible so that she can come down and live near us. There's a perfect flat for sale, just a five-minute's walk away, really ideal for her and we don't want to lose it."

This much personal detail after a seemly diet of weather and cricket usually led to some sort of request beginning with "I wonder if you would mind ...?"

We drew the line at minding the dog or the baby for half an hour whilst our customer popped down the road to Marks & Spencer.

"So we have to clear the house," he continued.

"Yes, I see."

"My mother-in-law has more or less chosen the furniture she wants to keep. There are some quite nice pieces, though most things will be too big for the flat, of course."

"Of course."

"So they're going to sell the rest."

"Very sensible."

"Those old wardrobes are enormous."

"They usually are."

"I'm told that furniture restorers break them up and use all that lovely old wood to patch up antiques."

"Yes, I believe they do."

"Shame, really."

He paused and looked around him for inspiration.

"The thing is …" he started and stopped. "The thing is, the house is full of his old books and we haven't a clue what to do with them. They're not leather-bound or anything. Just old books and I was wondering if you would mind …? Could you, by any chance? I can't think of anybody else."

The request faded into embarrassment.

We had certainly had more flattering requests to view or to give our expert opinion. Still, with the wisdom of Mark Twain, we faced the invitation with alacrity in our hearts and reluctance on our faces. It did not do to show the quickening of the pulse, the surge of excitement yet again, at the unlikely prospect of finding that elusive early Auden tucked between two battered paperbacks by Agatha Christie or an early unpublished poem by Wordsworth. The imagination knows no limits.

"What do you mean by 'just old books'? Are they just old paperbacks?" The voice is perfectly neutral.

"No, he didn't like paperbacks. There are a lot of pamphlets and foreign books, too."

"Well, I suppose we could have a look." The bookseller's voice slowed to suggest the possibility of a favour bestowed.

"That would be splendid!" he clapped his hands. "My wife is up there with her mother. I am sure they would give you lunch."

"Up there?"

"Yes, didn't I tell you? The house is just outside Leeds."

"No, as a matter of fact, you forgot to mention it. In that case, I am not sure."

"Oh, please go. It's only a hop up the motorway."

Of course we would go. Nothing would stop us. Who can resist a house full of unidentified books and mysterious pamphlets? So a few days later, the boot full of empty boxes ready to be filled with treasures untold, we set off for Leeds.

It was a modest, tidy, detached house on the outer outskirts of Leeds, almost in the country. There was the traditional layout of the suburban house built between the wars; entrance hall, door to the living room on the left, kitchen at the end of the hall and the downstairs lavatory tucked under the stairs. There were bookcases against almost every wall, plain utility shelves with no purpose other than to support the weight of books. No breakfront bookcases in polished mahogany. In fact, there was little beyond the utilitarian in the whole house, just plain curtains, plain armchairs and plain rugs to throw over cold knees in the winter. In the living room there was a two-bar electric heater. In the bedroom there was no such luxury.

We glanced to right and left as we were greeted by the mistress of the house and her daughter. Our hearts sank with disappointment; row upon row of books published by book clubs in the 1930s and again from the 1950s onwards, all in uniform binding, some cloth, some plastic disguised as leather with trompe-l'oeil raised bands and gilt scrolls bleeding into the sad plastic. Not publications to set the bookseller humming with joy.

The living room yielded a couple of interesting books on flying and a shelf or two of first editions, corners battered and missing their dust jackets. The empty boxes stayed put in the car. We glanced at each other. We would accept a quick lunch, then make our way back to London and home. You can't win them all. You have to try. Must never pass up an opportunity. Faint heart never won. That's the nature of the business. We rolled out the comforting clichés at each other and shrugged.

Upstairs we decided to separate, each one doing two bedrooms. The "best" books were usually kept downstairs and given the quality of what we had found so far, it was unlikely that the bedrooms would need more than a cursory ten minutes each.

The books had been stacked on the beds in uneven piles. There were small boxes of pamphlets on the floor, each bed a slag heap of fascist literature, apology, theory, propaganda, philosophy and history going back to the 1920s in English, German, Italian and Balkan languages we did not immediately identify. There were a few in Hungarian. There were pamphlets, explaining with scientific precision, with charts and diagrams, how Jews' ears were non-Aryan, especially the lobes. There was data on the cancer that was the Roma community in a well-ordered state. There was philosophy laid out in paragraphs, pages, chapters, the arguments so well structured it was difficult to remember the quagmire of the original premise. The memory of the philosophy when applied by the well-ordered state sent shivers down the spine. There was half a bedful of economics. There were pamphlets aimed at children and young people, so much of it attractive. Patriotism is such a beautiful word. There were pictures of laughing youth, healthy and fair, walking through forests. The call to join them was loud and irresistable. It was the "sound bite" of the pamphlets that was the most astonishing: one truth, one foolproof construction of evidence, one conclusion. Odium omnia vincit.

We had no time to sit and read extensively. That we did later. It was the odd page here and there, written by authors whose names we had never heard of, that struck us both. Der nationalsozialistische Staat, Mit Hitler an die Macht, Deutsche Menschen – deutsche Führer, all well-thumbed and so often read. On reading a lot more, it was the quiet logic, the absolute certainties, so certain that they did not need justification, just setting down clearly to enlighten those still in the dark, that shocked. There seemed to be no counterarguments to be examined and eventually disproved. They were not even mentioned. The holy writs of the major religions seemed pliable in comparison.

We were unqualified to set a value on this collection by any professional standards. We had no idea of the market value of a signed first edition of Mein Kampf, even an association copy dedicated to Dr Mengele. At every other level we were only too well qualified and we knew, without a word being exchanged, that we had to get these books out of the house and into hiding before they became the British National Party's reference library.

Ruth and I came out of our respective bedrooms round-eyed. We went downstairs to eat with the recently widowed mother and her distracted daughter. We attempted little bursts of conversation. There were obviously some things we wanted to know: were we looking at the collection of a dedicated academic historian or a fanatic? Were mother and daughter aware of the nature of the hoard and were they of the same persuasion?

"Did your father write a lot?"

"My father? Write? What makes you think that?"

"Well, you know, so many books, we thought maybe he had written one or two himself." A jocular reply with no particular logic to it.

"My father was hard put to write a letter. He just read a lot."

So that was one theory eliminated. We concentrated on the lettuce and cold ham, trying to think up questions that might lead us to where we wanted to go. After all, we could hardly ask, "Madam, was your father (or husband) a fundamentalist fascist with a heart of stone?"

"So your father was interested in Modern History?" Nice one. That is the sort of blanket question that could be stretched from the Somme to Marshal Tito by way of Prohibition.

"A bit. He seemed to think that nothing really worthwhile had happened in the world since 1944."

"1944?"

"I always thought it was an odd date for him to choose but he wasn't a great one for talking, was he, Mum?"

"Odd, as you say." It was difficult to prod her on yet keep our interest under firm control. The mother sat, her head bowed, contributing nothing to the conversation, cutting her lettuce into ever smaller pieces.

"That was towards the end of the war." There was no arguing with that, and she didn't.

"Yes, he said that Europe had taken a wrong turn and taken the world with it."

"So he was interested in politics?" Were we getting somewhere?

She burst out laughing. "What on earth gives you that idea? He didn't vote for as long as I can remember. He said that they were all wet, every man jack of them, without ideology."

"What! Not even the Labour Party?"

"No, he said that they were all as useless as each other. But we didn't talk about that sort of thing really. He said it wasn't for women to talk about but I think he had a few half-baked ideas of his own that kept him tight-lipped whenever our friendly politicians bobbed up upon TV. May have been a closet Communist for all I know," shrugged the daughter.

Her mother looked up startled.

"Oh no, dear, nothing like that. Not Daddy. He thought Communists were very misguided. Not good people at all." Her hands fluttered nervously to brush away the very idea. Blasphemy had been uttered at her table and she rushed in to calm the furies that may have been dispatched from the local cemetery as a result.

So we had our answer. The mother was aware of her husband's convictions and maybe even shared them. The daughter did not have a clue. We wondered how much the son-in-law knew but we never found out. He never came back to the shop.

We thanked them both for their delicious lunch and went back upstairs. We sat down in one of the bedrooms. We needed a little time to think. We were not qualified to value the books, true, but there was no way that we were going to leave them. We were not even going to rough guess their value on the open market because that was one market that this pile of venom was never going to see. So, we calculated that the daughter's interest was to get the books out of the house as a part of the clearance operation. The mother, who probably had a good idea what was lurking at the top of the stairs, was not going to haggle and risk drawing her daughter into the transaction. So we prepared to make an offer, not professional, not based on any expertise, but an honourable one. We saw ourselves more as undertakers than booksellers, ready to remove a putrid corpse out of the house.

We will never know if our offer was derisory. The mother accepted before we had come to the end of the sentence. The daughter was delighted.

"You will take them away now, won't you? Then we can get rid of all those awful shelves and the beds as well. It would be such a help."

We stacked the books in the basement of the shop, the section cordoned off, closed to the public. We had plenty of time to examine the hoard. We could not and did not try to trace the identity of the authors, the history of the publishing houses or the printers. We did not collate and we did not catalogue. We made no attempt to discover the market value of these masterpieces of perversion.

Over a short period we passed them on to safe hands.

Fortunately, there are many expeditions that we enjoyed on altogether a lighter note.

"I have to go to Glasgow next week, just for the day. Do you want to come?" said my husband. I had never been to Scotland, so I was delighted. I admit that a book hunt was not what immediately sprung to mind. I had assumed, wrongly, that once his business appointment was over, we would have the rest of the day to explore the city together. I had not asked and he had not told me that he had a series of meetings organised.

"What time shall we meet and where?" I asked blithely.

"Oh, you'd better make your own way back to the airport. Try to be there by seven, will you?"

And he disappeared through the handsome swing doors to his first appointment.

So I walked for a couple of hours, looking at the monuments and prescribed points of interest. Then I had a coffee and walked for another hour. The afternoon promised to stretch interminably.

This had not been intended as Glendale outing so I had not done any homework. Where in Glasgow were the antiquarian booksellers situated? I did not have my ABA Directory with me and until I found an antiquarian bookseller, I was not going to be able to put my hands on one. A Catch-22 situation. So I thought that the best place to ask was in a good bookshop selling new books. I had learnt to avoid the word "antiquarian": in the past a simple question had brought some surprising and surprised answers.

"Antiquwhat?"

"What do you want one of those for, a nice lady like you?"

"Oooh, there's posh then. D'you mean the boxes of stuff they put outside Oxfam?"

"If you mean 'second-hand' why don't you bloody say so?"

So I did. I went into a smart bookshop and asked a smart young man behind the counter if he knew where I could find a second-hand bookshop, a simple question simply put.

"What do you mean?" his accent was all but impenetrable to my southern ears but the expression was not. He looked taken aback.

"Used books," I said. "Are there any shops that sell used books?"

"There are," he said but offered no further information.

"And could you tell me where I could find them?" I prodded whilst I retrieved a small city map from my pocket. "I've never been to Glasgow before so I don't know my way around. Is there an area where there are few shops within walking distance of each other? That would be a great help."

He snatched the map from my hand and marked two crosses on the other side of the city.

"You'll find them if you look," he said vaguely and turned away to deal with other matters.

I thanked him for his help and left but he did not turn round.

I found the first shop with difficulty. The window did not carry a single book and the door was locked.

"RING" it said on a scruffy card stuck next to a chipped bakelite bell which looked like an invitation to instant electrocution. I thought that the stock must be rare and valuable to warrant such precautions. We certainly did not keep our shop door locked down in London.

I was ushered in by a shabby old man who wasn't really that old but who had shuffled into old age by neglecting every possible aspect of his appearance. His baggy trousers were held up by old-fashioned braces, his collarless shirt was less than fresh, to put it mildly. He was unshaven and wisps of mud grey hair brushed his shoulders.

"Canterbury Tales!" I thought and grinned at him. He did not grin back.

"I was told that you sold used books," I said.

"So?"

"Second-hand," I added, for the sake of clarity. "I wondered if I might come inside and take a look."

He shrugged and opened the door.

There wasn't a book to be seen, or bookshelf for that matter.

"Would it be possible for me to look around?"

"Look as much as you like."

"At the books, I mean."

He bent down behind the counter and heaved up a large cardboard box.

"This the sort of thing you looking for, then?" he asked smoothly.

I have to admit that I had never seen hard porn before and I doubt if it comes much harder than the pile of magazines presented for my delectation. They were all second-hand, though some of them had obviously passed through many more hands than two.

I must have gone very red. He smirked at me quite openly. My discomfiture turned to anger and that has always served me very well.

"Not exactly," I admitted. "This is all rather old hat though, isn't it?"

It was his turn to be taken aback. Still, I did not want him to produce a box of bestiality or other morsels for my obviously discriminating eye.

"I'll take this one," I said. "Five pounds do you?"

He took the note in disbelief. I took the magazine and fled.

"Did you have a good day?" asked my husband at the airport.

"Interesting," I conceded.

"Find anything?"

"You could say so."

Later that night, the children safely in bed, I produced my purchase. On the front cover was a close-up photograph of a gentleman's private part rampant for action.

"There you are. That's what I was offered when I asked for second-hand books."

"Really? How very odd," said my husband, holding the picture at arm's length. "I could swear I was at school with him."

On a more acceptable and respectable occasion, Ruth and I were invited to look at the books of the Polish government in exile. These were stored in a beautiful house in Knightsbridge and we had been asked if we would care to make an offer on those their guardians considered surplus to their requirements. We were greeted by two very elderly gentlemen, immaculately dressed, white shirts gleaming, ties knotted high on the throat. They addressed each other as "Count" and "Colonel" respectively, in the third person, in a Polish so courtly that it had probably never been heard outside the more ancient archives of the BBC World Service. It is a language I still speak fluently, an elegant pre-war version, but this was the

Polish of Mickiewicz and I was taken aback. The gentlemen bowed their heads. Lips hovered the prescribed two centimeters over our outstretched hands. My father kissed my hand on my birthday to acknowledge my status as a married woman, before giving me a bear hug to acknowledge my status as his daughter. Nobody else had ever done anything so un-British to my hand. I saw Ruth flush with pleasure; she had obviously experienced this particular homage amongst the gentlemen of her parents' circle in Paris and she obviously liked it, sophisticated lady!

We were invited to inspect the books laid out for us in neat piles. The subject matter was outside our field, mostly the history of Eastern Europe in the first half of the twentieth century. We quickly became so absorbed that we decided to make a modest offer for the lot, about 300 books, and study them at our leisure. A few of the books were in English, the rest were in Polish, Russian and other Slavonic languages I did not immediately identify. There were a good few in German and these I pushed along to Ruth. The Second World War and its immediate aftermath took up the whole of the second table.

I was born in Poland a few months before the war broke out, and the images in front of me were the stuff of my childhood. It was difficult to look at them and maintain a professional calm. Ruth had been smuggled out of Vienna by her father, leaving her mother behind for reasons judged to be best at the time, to the supposed safety of France just before the war exploded. There she stayed, hidden in the country, Colette or Paulette for the kind people who harboured her, but always Ruth for her father.

The triumphant photographs of smiling German soldiers trampling in burnished boots over Poland did not evoke the same memories for her but caused the same distress. We would indeed have to examine some of these books at our leisure, if leisure be the word.

We returned to the two gentlemen sitting in their office, both of us pensive and a little subdued. They were waiting for our decision. They sprang to their feet with spry alacrity. We explained that though the books were outside our specialised field of interest we would like to make an offer, since we found them very interesting and there were just enough books there to open a small new section in our basement.

"We have not had the pleasure of a visit to your establishment," said the Count.

"Then I hope you will come soon," said Ruth.

"We would advise when we would come. Our presence here is not essential on all days of the week, so an arrangement could be constructed which would permit us to come." said the Count.

"Oh, there is no necessity to advise us. The shop is open every day and we will be pleased to see you at any time you might choose to come." Ruth was picking up the courtly formality fast. Had she been speaking her native French, she would have dipped into the imperfect subjunctive.

"Then that will be our extreme pleasure and we shall organise such a visit at the earliest possible date."

And we all bowed and nodded to each other.

We had decided to make a fairly modest opening offer.

"Excellent, most excellent!" said the Count and he beamed his satisfaction.

Ruth and I looked at each other bewildered. It was unheard of for an offer to be accepted without the least discussion, a little bargaining, a grimace of disappointment. The most gently-born grandmother bringing her books to the shop would counter our opening offer with "I was hoping to get a little more for them." or "Do you think you could possibly do a little better?"

Our offer to the two Polish gentlemen was too low. It was not an honest offer, just an opening gambit towards one, but the guardians of the library did not know the rules of the game. The Colonel may, in a previous life, have bought wine for his regiment but he had never questioned the price. The Count had never haggled; perhaps he had once had a steward or a major-domo? As they smiled at us, we realised that for them both, business was an unpleasant foreign country. We, however, felt uncomfortable.

"That's just for the books on the big table." said Ruth brightly. "We could make a further offer for the books on the smaller table."

She thought fast on her feet, did Ruth. The Colonel waved a hand in response, a gracious gesture. The distasteful matter was to be pursued no further.

"Excellent! Most excellent." repeated the Count and the transaction was considered settled.

"Do you wish my secretary to send a cheque to this address?" Ruth asked without batting an eyelid.

Normally, it would not have been considered acceptable to take away books before paying for them. We had brought some cash along as a matter of course, yet to stand before the Count and the Colonel counting out twenty-pound notes, however pristine their condition, crisp from the bank, would have felt like a breach of some mysterious protocol. To plunge a hand into a bag and pull out a wad of money would offend.

Ruth, who had the money in her bag on this occasion, obviously felt the same because she kept it slung over her shoulder firmly shut, offering the services of her secretary instead. The secretary, for her part, made a mental note to include a "With Compliments" card and not to use an envelope from the Electricity Board, recycled with a sticky label.

"And now," said the Colonel, "perhaps the ladies would join us in a light luncheon?"

The ladies were pleased to do so. One of the desks was cleared at once. The Colonel opened a deep drawer and took out four champagne flutes with one practised swoop. The Count returned from an alcove tucked behind a curtain with a bottle of chilled champagne.

"We shall drink a toast," he announced solemnly. He opened the bottle with one push of the thumb and a discreet pop. I wondered if the toast would involve tossing the glasses into the fireplace.

"Szanowne Panie. Gracious ladies," said the Count, raising his glass.

"Szanowne Panie," echoed the Colonel.

This was champagne, not vodka, to be sipped with respect, not downed with bravado. The glasses were set down on the table. The gracious ladies in their turn raised their glasses and simpered. Then, both gentlemen opened their briefcases and brought out two large plastic boxes. Each box contained neatly packed sandwiches, the crusts trimmed. The napkins offered were of embroidered linen.

The conversation turned to our bookshop, how we had started, how we organised our working lives. The gentlemen listened with attention, both leaning slightly forward.

"Such a pleasant occupation for two married ladies," said the Count.

"Yes," pursued the Colonel, "it must give your husbands much serious satisfaction that you have chosen such an occupation. Books are a worthy pastime for ladies."

I held my breath lest the word "bookey" should bob up. My temper sometimes has an uncontrollable life of its own.

"Isn't it a small part dangerous? Any person could walk into the shop," said the Count.

"I don't think that anybody has ever been held up at gunpoint for their antiquarian books!" Ruth laughed.

"But yes, still," frowned the Count and drew in his lips. He shot his cuff and then folded his hands piously on his lap; having pointed out the danger, duty was done.

"And there have never been unfortunate circumstances?" the Colonel asked. There had been quite a few but modesty prevailed. We shook our heads.

"And who will you be sending to collect the books on your behalf?" asked the Colonel. "It would be wise to inform us, of course, so that we are both present to supervise the packing and dispatching."

Here was something else that had not occurred to us. Young and strong, we packed and carried our own boxes of books, most of the time.

Sometimes it took a little longer and we were exhausted and smelt of skunk, but whereas Ruth could draw on the services of a phantom secretary, she could not produce a real Glendale porter.

"I am afraid," said the Count sadly, "we shall not be of great assistance. We have old backs, too worn out by time to carry heavy things."

"Oh, of course not. No, that would be unthinkable," I protested. "We shall organise transport and call you to make sure that it's convenient."

Why could we not, quite simply, state that we packed and carried our own books? These very elderly aristocrats were imposing their world view on us and we both sat with ramrod backs, simpered prettily, and allowed ourselves to become too dainty and too feeble to pack some three hundred books and could not sully our fingers to pay for them. We were all but rustling our crinolines when we stood up to leave.

Ruth and I returned to our shop as if we were descending to a lower sphere.

"The sons?" asked Ruth.

"Can we afford them?" I asked.

Having realised that they had the monopoly of humping heavy boxes of books when we really could not manage alone or needed to get things done quickly, they behaved like every efficient cartel, fixed their prices and grinned at us. Sons just don't come cheap.

There is many a celebrity who came into our shop with an aggressive little question mark suspended over their head. It signalled quite clearly "Do you know who I am?" This goes with a facial tic that tells you to show your recognition, a smidgin of obsequious pleasure, and then to put your head down because the Famous Person must not be harassed.

So when the quite unremarkable man, without the celebrity question mark, came into the shop a couple of weeks later and asked if we had anything interesting on the Second World War, Ruth suggested he have a look in the basement on the shelves marked WW II, just to the left of the stairs. He came back upstairs about an hour later with a good half a dozen books. Whilst Ruth prepared the invoice, he ambled over to look at the Modern First Editions.

"Where did you get all those WW II books? They're a real find for me. I'm looking for background material for my next book."

He glanced back at the Modern First Editions and added, "I see you have three of mine."

Ruth paused, looked at him and sighed. Camus he wasn't. Eliot, Auden and Isherwood had all gone the same way. Was he going to be all hurt, whoever he was, because as far as she was concerned, he could be anyone who merited a place on the shelf and was still alive and male?

"And you've put a decent price on me but then, you've got the dust jackets."

Ruth looked desperately along the shelves, but we prided ourselves on the condition of the modern first editions, so the majority of the books were complete with their dust jackets, that was no help.

"You'll have to forgive me ..." she said.

"Certainly."

With her French accent at full throttle she continued, "... but my partner specialises in English literature. I deal with French and Continental literature."

She waved her hand vaguely towards Europe.

"I see." he nodded.

"So I don't quite know who you are," she added, peering at him, as if a small hint might identify him as an efficient translator of French or Continental literature and so just within her domain.

"I gathered." he said seriously.

"I don't really look at the photographs on the dust jackets." she added.

"Neither do I." he said.

"Will you give me your name? I need it for the invoice."

Let there be no suspicion of vulgar curiosity.

"If you tell me yours."

Reluctantly, she did.

He took three books from the shelf and wrote "For Ruth, with good wishes, Len Deighton."

When eventually Funeral in Berlin was published, Ruth felt that a small corner of it was hers.

Sometimes, when we did not want to buy a book, or a box of books on offer, we seemed to bring out the worst in the prospective vendor.

"I think I'd better have a word with the manager," was common enough.

The unwanted book was left on the desk for the manager's inspection. The phantom manager was then dispatched on holiday, was ill in hospital, had given in his notice or whatever fate Ruth and I threw at him. The non-existent manager was, obviously, a man.

Or else, the price we offered was far below the vendor's expectations.
"But my brother-in-law told me ..."

"You must be joking! Look at all the gold on the sides of the pages. It must be worth a fortune."

"That's daft. This was published in 1863, so it's a real antique, you know, properly old."

"Come on, only one volume is missing. There are fourteen left."

"It belonged to my grandmother."

"What do you mean by shaky?"

"I'm selling this for an old age pensioner who can't get out and about any more."

"I can see you've got one here that's almost exactly the same and you're asking double."

So we, in our turn, made a list of reasons why we could not buy the books offered. Most of them were greeted with a sneer.
"I'm afraid we're not buying in this category at the moment."

"This is very specialised. I think you'd be better off selling it through one of the major auction houses." (Let Sotheby's deal with the missing volume. Their back is broader.)

None of the reasons we offered always let us off the hook; a hardened vendor could make us feel like a crook or a worm for not buying his books.

He could and did stand with an icy stare waiting in complete silence and wait for you to give the real reasons why you didn't want to buy his carton of Dickens in too many parts or box of wine books that looked as if they had done some degustation on their own account. At least, we never told him that we didn't have the time, that we'd read them all, to come back on Saturday. And we never whispered that we loved his books but we would have to ask an omnipotent husband.

Chapter 6 ½

We read the papers, listened to the news, lived a life outside the world of Glendale. I wrote poems which Ruth gathered.

   SONGS MY MOTHER NEVER TAUGHT ME
Anthem for Ireland, to be chanted by any lisping Belfast child against the background of some sweetly pretty hymn tune.

HAIL MARY,
FULL OF GRACE,
WHY'RE THEY SPITTING
IN YOUR FACE?
WHILE THE THIRTY-NINE ARTICLES
FRAGMENTS AND PARTICLES
LODGED IN MY EYE AND IN MY ARSE.
WHAT A FARCE.

GENTLE JESUS
MEEK AND MILD

SACRIFICE
ANOTHER CHILD?
WHILE THE ANGELS ARE SINGING
ANTHEMS AND CANTICLES
DRINK THE BLOOD, RAISE THE HOST
HERE'S THE TOAST.

RAISE YOU GLASS TO THE PROVOS
RAISE YOUR EYES TO SINN FEIN
LOWER YOUR HAND
FOR PROTECTION'S
A NEW IRISH GAME.
THE PEACE LIES IN PIECES
AND THE PIECES ARE SCATTERED
WHILE THE PROVOS ARE PROVING
AND APPRENTICE BOYS
MOVING
AND MARCHING IN ORANGE
AND PREACHING THE GREEN
IN YOUR NAME
BEATING PRAYERS
IN THE HILLS AND THE VALES
DOMINUS TECUM---
BUT WHOM SHALL WE SEEK?

HOLY MARY,
MOTHER OF GOD
TARRED AND FEATHERED
ON THE ALTAR
WHILE THEY ARE SNIPING YOUR PRAISES
FROM SANCTIFIED PLACES
IN ARMAGH AND FALLS ROAD,
GRACE BESTOWED.

FORGIVE US OUR TRESPASSES
REMEMBER OUR SINS
GOD'S ASLEEP IN HIS HEAVEN.
CAN ANY MAN WIN?
(1976)

CONCORD

I saw an angel in the sky
On wings of steel come gliding by,
With beady eyes, proud look unholy,
And, for an heavenly body, slowly,
I asked the reason for his mood.
He found the question somewhat crude.

"Beelzebub has long departed
While heav'n, razed by a humanist inferno
Is smouldering yet; it's hard to go
Across philosophies uncharted.
Why, I've even heard it said
That, somewhere, God is lying dead."

With swept back wings & nose semitic,
Struggling to pre-empt each new critic,
He finds fresh flaws in fellowship
Just trying to find a landing strip.

I saw an angel in the sky
On wings of steel come listing by,
Looking for a brand new home,
A comprehensive aerodrome.

October 2nd 1976

ODE TO A LADY AT CROIX VALMER

Lady Penelope Winston Jones
Sat on the beach at Croix Valmer
And with her usual savoir faire
Removed her bra
To show the local ladies that
An Englishwoman in a hat
Displaying two fried eggs on toast
Can still compete and even boast

That though the Empire may be lost
A lady can retain her frost,
For years of Cheltenham will not thaw
Just because her tits are raw.

Sir Rodney ffeatherstonaugh Winston Jones,
Though squirming to his very bones
To see his lady thus displayed
Took up his Times and gently made
A face of such Etonian derision
M'lady made a quick decision,
Reached for her bag without ado,
Replaced her bra, size 32.

The moral of this story is
That if you wish to have allure
When lying on the Côte d'Azur
Display your tits if French or Spanish,
A British brace it's best to banish.

To mark the official advent of the monokini in the South of France.

Written in September 1992 after listening to Desert Island discs. We ha small radio in the shop.

FIVE TREASURES FOR A DESERT ISLAND

I'll take my pillow first,
its feathers old, exhausted,
its linen slip threadbare.
At least when I'm asleep
I'll think I'm home.

I'll play Mozart's Figaro
until the disc is bald
and dare to croak along
where I cannot be heard
And rightly burnt for blasphemy.

I'll take an album
stuffed to the boards
with photographs of parents
sons and friends, each
Moment captured worth
A week, at least, of reverie.

I'll take Jane Austen,
Oxford Edition, with notes,
dust wrappers in cellophane,
a page or two a day
to keep the cold, hunger, thirst,
the loneliness, at bay.

I'll take the ruby ring
given with love and wit
so that, like Aladdin,
with the slightest rub,
I can conjure you, my genie.

PICKING MUSHROOMS
Poland 1944

They had names that slid
over the tongue---
Maslanki! Maslanki!---
and left a whispered trace.
The pan squatted its weight
across two gas rings
greasy black with goose dripping.
A bowl of eggs, new-laid, straw
smeared to the shells, a loaf of grey bread,
two plates, both chipped,
two forks, two mugs of milk
tepid from the cow
so thick with cream that they glowed yellow.
Ready.

And we were off across the fields,
clogs skimming wet grass,
the sun heaving its first heat
over the shading tops of trees,
into the forest.
Rabbits
Flashed us white rumps and fled.

We picked the red ones first,
white stems, white enamel dots,
toy mushrooms. Later I watched her
mash them into poison soup
to kill the blue fat flies
that bombed and buzzed us without rest,
and then I watched them
drink their fill and die,
Dying a hit-and-hit affair.

For us the satin brown ones,
covered with the night's fine spray,
waited in clumps,
their rounded table-heads tilted attention.
She told me how at dead of night
the elves cut with their elfin swords
a thousand cuts beneath each head;
tipped with their magic balm
they turned as innocent as my pink hand.
The rest, seeping their inky stains
Were cut by witches and purple goblins.
That's how I knew.
She, who kept me in fields
invisible from glass-blue eyes
of jackbooted warlocks
had told me so
and so I picked secure.

When both our baskets
were filled to the rim,
she took my hand

and we walked home,
hot sun pricking our backs,
the grass humming and dry.

The smell of forest mushrooms
sizzling in fat
the sound of eggs being beaten with a fork,
dark bread and milk and flies
and hot sun through dirty window panes
trip wires that sometimes leave me
tangled in doorways
or dazzled in market squares.

(Going back to a sweet moment in a difficult childhood, I left this for Ruth in the Day Book. I kept a copy for me, which was unusual.

Perhaps a book on Mushrooms inspired this one. Or perhaps it was the jackbooted warlocks in their immaculate uniforms, so prominent and so numerous in the books we bought from the two gentlemen in the Polish library. I can no longer remember.)

Chapter 7

*Selling books, including some dismal failures,
and wisdom acquired in the process*

"I'll give you £12."
Silence.
"You are so difficult to do business with and so nice to look at. Come on, you are not going to let me walk out without buying?"
Silence.
I did.

Where buying books to keep the shop stocked and ever-interesting presented one kind of challenge, selling presented quite another. There is no art or technique needed to sell old books; salesmanship can only get in the way. You cannot convince somebody looking for a first-edition Shakespeare that their lifestyle will be enhanced by three early Agatha Christies with dust jackets or that they will not be keeping up with the Joneses but that they will be The Joneses if they own the complete set of Encyclopaedia Britannica, 11th edition. It just doesn't work. Knowledge, information, humility in the presence of devout collectors, infinite patience, careful checking of editions and issues all help. Smooth, tutored salesmanship does not. The experienced salesperson who tells you how lovely you look whatever blobby size-8 garment you have stretched over your size-14 body, will not do in a bookshop.

On the other hand, people who do not have the least pang of conscience on leaving a shoe shop after having tried on fifteen pairs without even buying a shoehorn tend to look sheepish if they make their way towards the door without buying a book.

The reasons we were offered for not buying a book were noted in the Day Books over the years. They make a fine collection of the improbable, the impossible and the very imaginative. And the irritating beyond belief.

Being a woman, I suppose I was particularly irritated by the shy lady in a headscarf (and they were almost invariably modest of eye and wearing a silk headscarf) who reluctantly gave me back the book she had been fondling lovingly for ten minutes with the conspiratorial whisper, "It's no good. I'll have to ask my husband. It's such a lot of money."

Depending on our mood, we sometimes entered the conspiracy in our own fashion.

"Yes, I think you should. Husbands are so wise, don't you find? We do best when we leave such big decisions to them. For my part, I don't buy a tomato without phoning him first."

Just as lies should be whoppers, insolence should be delivered with the round-eyed innocence of a child. Ruth, whose eyes are blue and who has better control of her features, did insolence rather well.

The reverse situation never arose. Men bought what they wanted without hesitation and then said:

"Oh, for heaven's sake, find me an M & S bag to put it in. She'll kill me if I bring another book into the house."

It was difficult to imagine the mouse in the headscarf, having denied herself the pleasure of a book, standing at the front door ready to open his head because he was trying to smuggle one into the house. But then, perhaps men who buy books are married to ferocious wives in hats.

The price of a book, oddly enough, was rarely the first reason offered for not buying, though we do have a note about a man who came in looking for illustrated fairy tales. I remember him well, tall, with a good suit that had seen better days and the assurance of someone whose place in the universe is fixed beyond question.

"Ninety pounds!" he snorted. "But it's only for my wife!"

The ungovernable tongue suggested he come back when he was buying a present for his mistress. That, I suppose, is as near as I came to being slapped by a customer. We did not see him again.

As well as the lady in sable at the New York book fair, there was also another who came into the shop, jangling gold chains and bracelets, who found our shop just too cute. She peered at the faint pencil mark on the front end paper of a little book that had caught her fancy. She looked at it more closely and half whispered with awe:

"Fifteen English pounds? For a book? And it's not even nooo!"

There was another good lady who complained bitterly at the price we were asking and at last suggested we let her have it for half price because she only wanted the pretty leather outside part to make a cigarette box and we were welcome to keep the inside with all the words.

Another common reason offered for not making a purchase as the failed customer slipped sideways out of the door was a lack of time. I wish we had had a shiny pound coin for every time we heard:

"I just wish I had more time. You have such a lovely shop. One really needs to spend half a day here. Are you open on Saturday/Sunday/Thursday?"

It would have bumped up the week's takings considerably.

People didn't buy books because the binding was the wrong colour or the size was too big/small. They didn't buy because they had read them all (followers of the lies should be whoppers philosophy) or because it was light and warm in our basement and the red leather armchairs were comfortable. Why buy a book if you can settle in the shop and read it there?

That is how we met Milena.

Milena was a refugee from Prague who had slipped out under the wire during the Velvet Revolution. She had been married, but that was in another life. Now she was married again to a nice Englishman, very good to her but a bit mean with money. He did not want her to work because with her imperfect English she could not hold down a job worthy of his dignity and no wife of his was going to be a waitress or some such. She had cleaned her house, prepared his tea and wandered round the West End of London gazing at dresses and electric mixers and leather armchairs she could not buy. Her nice husband gave her money on a daily basis. Should she need a pair of tights or a tube of toothpaste, she had to propose the item on the day's list which she presented straight after breakfast; what he did not approve of he simply crossed out and deducted the cost from the day's allowance.

She found us by chance, and having found us, we became her refuge. She explained and apologised immediately that she could not buy a book. The reason why, however, came a great deal later. Never did she complain about the financial arrangements imposed by her husband.

"In my country, I worked. Everybody has to work to buy food and coal and shoes. Here, I am a fat do-nothing bee so I have no money."

It was difficult not to be a little indignant on her behalf but she seemed to find any rule made by her nice, English husband acceptable. His money. His rules.

She spent a long time in our basement reading. I don't think she meant to steal books, only to take them home to finish. We did suspect that she was walking out with books she had not paid for but we had no proof until one day one fell out of the pocket of the dress she wore under her heavy coat.

"Oh, sorry," she said, "that was a small bit careless, wasn't it?"

We suggested that a public library was better suited to her needs than our little shop. And there they had a well-organised system for taking books home called, in English, the Lending Library.

"But I like it here so much," she said.

So she continued to come and as she was leaving she would open her coat and pat her pockets.

"Look! No books. I know Glendale not a public lending library."

But we were convinced that we continued to "lend" in her basket or handbag or shopping bag and somehow we failed to resent it.

Theft was a double problem for us. There was the problem of books stolen from us, what accountants sweetly call "shrinkage"; why they can't bring themselves to audit books with a bold "stock stolen" column, I have never understood. There was also the care that had to be taken not to buy books stolen from other booksellers or quite simply stolen.

There were some interesting techniques thieves used. There was a period, for example, when our in-house thief replaced books that he stole with something that looked vaguely similar in size so that there was never a tell-tale gap on the shelf. Days, perhaps weeks later, you would put your hand out for Houdini or Hoffmann and draw it back with volume four (of six) of forgettable sermons. This must have happened half a dozen times. Our list of suspects grew. We hovered like wasps over browsers. We put mirrors in strategic places. We watched hands even as we talked to faces (those old conjuring books teach you a thing or two about the hand moving faster than the eye). Our list of suspects narrowed. We bought a box of very old books in very foreign languages that looked the part, marked them at fairy tale prices and scattered them on the shelves. We waited. We noted carefully who looked at them. One customer looked at the price of one of our decoy ducks and burst out laughing. I explained primly that this was not one of my languages but I am sure that my partner had done her research correctly. The customer was not convinced and turned it over, to my infinite embarassement. I could see our reputation as serious antiquarian booksellers taking a dive. But within a week two of the decoys had disappeared. With relief we took the others off the shelves, knowing that our thief would learn at the first fence that we were completely unreliable suppliers of fine quality swag. No more books were stolen in this particular way.

Then there was the lanky fellow with sad clothes, too short at wrist and ankle. He always brought a book or two to sell and then went off to browse whilst we examined them. There seemed to be something admirably discreet about that. It gave us a chance to look at lists of stolen books, check plates, endpapers and prices. The books were never particularly valuable. Sometimes we bought and sometimes we returned the books with our apologies and thanks. Whatever price we offered to pay was never refused. His disappointment when we did not buy was almost tearful. Our suspicions grew but the books appeared clean. We were almost certain that he was stealing from us. His visits were regular and increasingly unwelcome and we stopped buying his books however inexpensive and attractive they appeared. He cross-examined us, but without aggression, just a whine, wanting to know why we wouldn't buy now what we had bought eagerly three months before. Somehow we couldn't bring ourselves to tell him not to come to the shop anymore. You can't condemn someone because your instinct tells you that they are offering you stolen property and what is more, even if you haven't seen them do it with your own eyes, you are certain that they are stealing from you. He didn't give us any grounds to warn him off. You can't tell someone to keep away because you don't like their face, unless you want to put your own in jeopardy that is. So we watched him come and go on his regular visits with increasing impatience and frustration.

My chance came when I saw him make a strange movement on the other side of the shop. When a customer has his back to you and is taking books off the shelves then putting them back again, the arm has a recognisable movement, a healthy up and down jerk of the elbow. When the book is being taken off the shelf and slipped into the front of the anorak, the angle of the elbow changes. The heart of the bookseller gives a thump of recognition and distress. My lanky friend had just lifted a book and I know that I am a devout coward. A rugby tackle was out of the question. I walked casually to the door of the shop and opened it, then, with imperious tones that owed everything to Edith Evans I commanded the young man to turn round. I stood firmly in the doorway, because if things were going to turn nasty I wanted a chance to make a run for it. The front of his anorak was suspiciously square. I told him to unzip it. He refused. I commanded again when the large, square book gave itself up of its own accord, slipped from the bottom of his anorak and fell to the floor. He fled past me as I stepped neatly to one side. Lady Bracknell seemed to evaporate with him for I found that my knees had gone strangely soft and my need for smelling salts and a fan reduced me to the level of Dickens' more irritating heroines. But I freely admit that I did feel a bit of a heroine, however feeble, and that is never to be encouraged. The only thing more tedious than a brand new heroine is someone who has recently had an operation. The modesty with which I told my tale was entirely false.

The way I handled the other major thief in our working lives leaves me much to be modest about. When a young man dressed in leathers and bearing a pristine copy of one bound volume of the Maîtres d'Affiche, as well as a motor-cycle helmet, came into the shop, my antennae twitched. There is no reason why people who ride motor bikes and wear dirty leathers should not be interested in posters or neo-Platonism or early Russian icons for that matter. One's choice of transport or political party or sexual orientation has no bearing on one's aesthetic sensibilities. So there. I accused my antennae of intellectual snobbery and gave the young man my full attention. He did not know the difference between Mucha and the Daily Mirror. I asked him if he could give me some proof of ownership. He told me that he had been left the book by his grandfather and that his brother had another volume and that he, too, wanted to sell. The grandfather came across more as a Steptoe than a Berenson. He told me about china teapots, fireplaces and the kind of drawings that one couldn't possibly show a lady, though he did want to sell those as well. He blushed, he laughed, he prattled about old Pa, he was completely at ease so that I was distracted and forgot to pursue the request for proof of ownership. He agreed readily when I suggested he go away for half an hour to give me a chance to look at the posters and work out a price. He left his helmet and went off cheerfully. I rang the usual places and checked the usual lists but there was no mention of the books having been stolen. When he came back we haggled amicably. He asked for cash but he was hardly the first perosn to do so. I agreed to buy his brother's book as well, for the same price. He signed a name with a flourish on the receipt I had prepared.

When the police came (three officers, one for each book and one for us), the books were on display, as if waiting for them. Our young man had lifted the books from an art gallery which explained why there was no mention of them on any of our lists. These were issued by our professional body and we consulted them openly whenever we were offered a book, especially by a private individual we did not know. Unfortunately, the list did not cover books stolen from other organisations. The gallery owner refused to believe that we had bought the books in good faith, in spite of our clearance by the police and refused to split the cost of the loss with us. This was taken for granted in the book trade, but then, he was not in the book trade. He was also very rude. Since the property could not be released to him by the police without our signature, he was persuaded; the loss was considerable but at least, when shared, we each only suffered half.

Then, there was Veronique. She didn't pour out her story in storms of indignation, but let it seep out drop by drop and we never did find out how it all ended. With her red hair bundled into a loose knot at the nape of her neck, the pale creamy skin of redheads, she was, I suppose, almost pretty. She played on the French accent to put Maurice Chevalier to shame. At first she used to wander in and just look around. Then she chose a small inexpensive children's book and asked me about it. When she realised that Ruth was French she came more often and stayed a little longer.

She wanted to learn as much as possible about children's books because she wanted to start a collection for her daughter. She wasn't going to show it to her at once because it was going to be a surprise for her when she was older and could appreciate it. Her daughter spent the weekends in the country. Her daughter had a pony. Her daughter had a tree house. Her daughter went to such a wonderful little school in Knightsbridge, such a wonderful part of London, where she made such wonderful little friends... We asked if she would like to bring her daughter to the shop because most children found it a magic place with its old fashioned books and games. Their visits were sometimes heavy on fragile bindings but they seemed to know instinctively that they were handling things that once belonged to those very children shown in the illustrations with their pantaloons and huge hula hoops. Veronique, however, was startled by the suggestion.

"Oh no," she said, "I couldn't do that. We never go out together."

"Why not?" was the obvious question. But there was no reply. Veronique carried on looking at books as if the question had not been asked.

For several months she did not come to the shop and then she reappeared, smiling, with a beautifully bound copy of pochoir illustrations by Leon Bakst for the Ballet Russes. The book was in pristine condition in its original box. The colours glowed. The book was signed by Bakst and dedicated to a princely patron of the ballets. Veronique wished to sell it. The first question was to ask for its provenance because though Veronique had been coming to the shop for many months there had never been any indication that she had a book of this calibre in her possession. The books she had bought for her daughter had not been expensive. The price had barely crept into double figures. There was room for a little disquiet.

"Oh," she answered without the least hesitation, "this was my mother's. She has a small collection and she has given everything to me, last month, when I went to visit her. For my daughter. But I want to sell and get beautiful children's books for her. More interesting for a little girl, don't you think?"

"So you do want to sell this then?" Ruth asked, a little more eagerly than her usual haggling skills should have allowed.

"Yes, yes. You want to buy it?"

"We may be interested."

Ruth retreated to the stance of reluctant buyer, the best negotiating position when dealing with sellers not in the trade. It didn't wash with the professionals.

Ruth examined the book from every angle, trying to find the least flaw which could warrant a sniff and a slight curl of the lip. There was none.

"Well," she said limply, "it is of very limited interest. Ballet, you know, everybody's cup of tea." She waited to be laughed out of court.

"But the pictures are very pretty, aren't they?" Veronique answered anxiously.

It would appear that she knew nothing of Leon Bakst or the Ballet Russes. Ruth offered a low price, just within the bounds of honesty but only just. But it was a lot of money. Veronique opened her eyes wide and there was a sharp intake of breath. Ruth had expected this to be the opening gambit in a long negotiation which should have started with

Veronique putting a proprietary hand on her book and telling Ruth not to be ridiculous. She should then have demanded double and set the ball rolling back and forth in the best tradition.

"As much as that?" she gasped. "I'll take it."

"Well, if you're sure," said Ruth feeling awkward.

"Yes. Please. I want cash."

This was not an unusual request and the reasons were not necessarily to evade tax. Sometimes it was husband or wife evasion. And within the trade we suspected that there was a certain amount of dishonest trading behind the backs of unloved associates locked in uneasy partnerships. So when Veronique asked for cash, we did not bother to wonder why. From the impressive stash of twenty-pound notes she took two to spend on the next children's book for her daughter's collection. The rest she tucked into the inside pocket of her ample brown coat and left the shop on wings.

She came more often. She bought a pretty little book every now and again but nothing to the value of the book she had sold us. We did notice however, that she had a few new clothes.

Over the next two years she brought some twenty books which we bought eagerly. In her turn she bought pretty Victorian children's books for her daughter but again, nothing to the value of the books which she sold. We reasoned sensibly that we were not the only bookshop in London so perhaps she was adding to her collection elsewhere.

The letter from the city firm of solicitors was on heavy bonded paper, the names of the partners embossed in black. It looked like an invitation to a wedding or notice of a recent death. The invitation, however, was to return the following twenty or so books to their client, post haste, their rightful owner, their client bearing a name that sounded like a whole shipping line in itself. The titles listed did not need to be cross-referenced in our files; from the first Bakst to the more recent Cocteau, every one of Veronique's little collection, given to her by her dear Maman, was there.

We were shocked. Most of the books had long been sold. We could trace most of them, certainly, but what then? The alternatives that we bounced off each other were grim, loss of reputation, financial difficulties. We began to have visions of the two of us standing side by side in the dock. There was no glimmer of hope. We scurried round to "our" solicitor, an old family friend. This was the first time that Glendale needed to think in the grandiose terms of "our" solicitor and the thought made us miserable. He calmed us down. We were both talking at once. He looked at the letter.

We told him that we had bought the books from a certain Mlle Veronique in the belief that they were her property, a gift from her mother.

"You bought these in good faith then." he stated.

"Yes!" we chorused.

"You paid a price which would be considered reasonable by your professional body?"

"Yes," we said, more quietly. "less than we would have paid at auction," we admitted, "but that is one of the benefits of having a shop, isn't it?"

He did not pursue that feeble logic.

"Look, you didn't pay a fiver for a Cartier watch, did you?"

"No nothing like that."

Our virtue was restored.

"Do you have a record of every transaction and did you give a receipt?"

"Yes!"

The chorus was back in tune. He decided that he would not reply on our behalf. We were to write the letter ourselves, informing the worthy solicitors that we were not acquainted with his client and that he should address his plaint to the police with whom we would co-operate fully on all matters. And that was the end of that. We never heard another word and the expected visit from the police never came.

We did not expect to see Veronique again but a few weeks later she came in as if nothing had happened, with no apology and no explanation.

"You took the books from Mr S.?" we asked, as if the question needed asking. "We could have been in serious difficulties, you know."

She shrugged.

"But you weren't, were you? And I needed the money." she said as if that explained and justified everything.

Veronique had had a very brief affair with Mr S. and unlike most affairs that end in an unwanted pregnancy, Mr S. wanted this little girl. He informed Veronique, who was very young and whose knowledge of English and Family Law was negligible, that in England the only way for him to acknowledge paternity was to adopt the child. So she signed papers right and left in front of lawyers and witnesses. Thereafter she was to live in the basement of his splendid London residence, act as a housekeeper and be with her daughter during the week in term time. She was not to take her daughter out of the house and its high-walled garden. Holidays were spent in Greece. At such times Veronique was free to visit her family in France if she so wished. Since he was now the child's legal parent, he would take her away and Veronique would not see her again if any of his edicts was disobeyed. She was given board, lodging and a small personal allowance.

He did not look at the books on his shelves from one year's end to the next. It had been so easy to take one out and shuffle the rest together so that the gap did not show. By the time she had taken twenty, he must have spotted the loss.

"He never opened one," she snorted, "so it couldn't be because he wanted to look at something. He only ever looks at that pink newspaper anyway. It was an investment. Everything is an investment. My daughter is an investment and when she is old enough he will marry her to somebody who has more ships in the next port."

She paused and glared at us fiercely as if the whole thing was our fault.

"Only, I sold his books and I had money for a solicitor. In England, he cannot steal my daughter. Now I know that."

After that, she did not come any more.

Apart from avoiding stolen books, we sold good books to interesting people. Some were more interesting than necessary for the running of the shop but there was no avoiding them. Our Italian was one such gentleman.

It's through circumstances rather than any great academic prowess that Ruth and I have a good grasp of some half a dozen languages between us. It has proved useful.

Whether in a shop or in a book fair, we admitted to nothing beyond English unless we were asked. If asked, however, we would willingly translate, interpret and help in any way we could. We helped customers book hotels. We helped colleagues through foreign bureaucracies. Two or three people walking into our stand or into our shop talking merrily in their own language about us or about our stock on the assumption that the lump behind the desk could not possibly have the wit to understand a word, were met with presumed witless incomprehension. I admit freely that there was an element of wounded pride in this stance. I admit even more freely that there was a lot of fun to be had.

Thus I learned that I had a perfectly dreadful haircut and should never, ever wear yellow. Ruth kept an impassive face when she overheard one customer inform another that Jack the Ripper's crimes were copycat murders taken from a story written by Sherlock Holmes. She learned that you could not get a good meal anywhere in London and that the streets behind the Grosvenor House Hotel were of a grinding poverty beyond belief. The slums of Mayfair? She put her head down and concentrated hard on the rubber at the end of her pencil.

The man was beautifully dressed, his flowing locks flawlessly shaped, no simple haircut at the hands of the local barber. The suit had a label sewn discretely on the outside of the cuff; such discretion is never bought cheaply. Signor Bussoni did not look at me. Signor Bussoni did not speak to me. He had a wisp of a flustered woman next to him and she communicated Signor Bussoni's desires and wishes in hysterical undertones. My replies were translated back into brave Italian. I could have done better but then, I had not been asked ...

An Italian completely devoid of charm is a rare creature. Perhaps Signor Bussoni reserved his for social occasions because his little interpreter was not granted a sliver for her pains. I was shown nothing at all.

"Ask her ...tell her ...I want ... bring me ... put it there ... I want the one on the top shelf ...I want invoices with two copies ... tell her ninety days and I'll pay her when I'm ready ..."

There is an excellent array of words for "please" and "thank you" in Italian. Per favore, per piacere, per cortesia, but Signor Bussoni seemed unaware of them.

The pile on my desk grew. Signor Bussoni looked at them with great satisfaction whilst I suspected that it would not be long before I would be putting them back on the shelves. The personal assistant fluttered and hovered. I added up the column of figures and handed her the total.

"Li prenderò ad ogni modo ma vedi un po' fin dove scende con il prezzo," he said.

"What discount do you offer?" she asked meekly.

"We offer a 5%-discount to the trade but I don't think that Mr Bussoni is a colleague."

"Oh no!" she looked quite shocked. "Signor Bussoni is not in trade. He is a lawyer. In Milan."

"I am afraid that in that case I am not permitted to offer any discount." She translated.

"Stupid woman. She hasn't a clue how to run a business. Everyone gives a discount."

She did not translate the whole comment, just the last sentence. I pleaded the helplessness of the employee; discount was outside my competence. She shrugged.

"Signor Bussoni wishes to have the books invoiced and sent to his office.

In Milan. The usual ninety days credit from the receipt of the books, he says."

"Usual?" I asked, looking as bewildered as a seriously bad actress who is not in the least bit bewildered, can manage.

"Oh, for heaven's sake," he snapped, "explain to her what 30, 90 and 120 days against invoice means."

The assistant began to explain. I interrupted, smiling kindly.

"Please tell Mr Bussoni that I am familiar with the procedure. Please convey to him that this credit is offered by pre-arrangement to known customers against previous references."

She struggled with that little lot into Italian. I put my hand with dignity on the pile of books and hoped that I could restrain the giggle a little longer. He glared at me.

"Oh, pay the stupid cow, give her my address and tell her to send them. Let's go, I've wasted enough time."

He produced a plump wallet and counted out the 50 pound notes with a practised thumb. He pushed them across the desk with disdain whilst the little woman ransacked her bag for his visiting card. I held it between two fingers and smiled at him.

"La deficiente La ringrazia e rimane a disposizione per future acquisti."

I thought he was going to kill me. Nasty.

Then there was the man who came in with the furrowed brow, a sheet of neatly folded A4 and a tape measure.

"I wonder if you could help?"

Ruth promised to try, her best helpful smile at the ready.

"I want to fill a shelf."

"Yes."

"With books."

"Oh good."

Given that there was a singular lack of lamb chops and crystal vases on display, Ruth found it difficult to keep the witty riposte in check.

"It's a metre long and thirty centimetres high," he said.

"What sort of books do you have in mind?"

He paused to give the matter a thought.

"Well, I like red ones best but the odd green or blue here or there would look nice."

Ruth got the picture. We had provided books and old valentines to set decorators both for films and television. They liked cloth covers for the serials and good worn leather for the country house costume dramas. Nothing easier.

"Will you be wanting them for long?" she asked.

"For long?"

"Yes, is it for a film or a play?"

"Oh, no," he said aghast. "It's for me. You know. My home. I have this shelf in an alcove and I think books will look really neat."

"They usually do." said Ruth. The witty riposte was bubbling towards the surface. She squashed it.

So she started to pull out books with fancy spines and fancy lettering, predominantly red, the odd blue one here and green one there and arranged them in some semblance of artistic disarray on the desk.

"Do you want them all vertical or shall we have a small stack here at the end, on their sides, at an angle?"

"Lovely idea," he said, "It makes it look kind of casual, doesn't it?"

"Yes," she agreed, "almost as if they had been read."

Ruth numbered the books for him lightly in pencil so that he would not muddle the order and make a mess of the colour scheme. So, a red cloth history of monasteries was to sit prettily next to an anthology of verse about cats and a nineteenth-century guide to Alpine inns, in green cloth, was to nestle next to a dark pink book of fairy tales for dolls and teddy bears. One metre of all sorts, nothing more than 30 cm high.

Her sigh in the Day Book was weary. Would it be wallpaper next?

There are collectors who collect books round their professions; lawyers who collect law books, doctors who collect medical books. Yet others collect material around their field of interest; cookery books for cooks, Victorian ballads for aspiring singers, philately for stamp collectors.

There are also those who collect material, be it books, memorabilia or ephemera around their identity. Australians asked for Australiana. The Irish most often asked for Irish authors and illustrators. And one lady from Malta who, inevitably, would buy anything that made any reference to Malta, however peripheral.

Orthodox Jews asked for Hebraica, Judaica. And then, just in case those words were too complicated, they asked if we had anything of Jewish interest.

Serious, slightly apologetic to be asking a woman and obviously one ignorant of the subject, they were incredulous and delighted if anything, however lowly, was offered.

A man came in, eyes modestly lowered, wearing all the trappings of the ultra-orthodox Jew, black suit, long curls hanging over his ears, hat tipped towards the back of his head, and beard. Before he had a chance to ask the question, I offered the answer.

"I am afraid we have no Judaica at all, at the moment."

He looked up at me, eyes twinkling.

"Judaica?" he said. "No. I'm not looking for Judaica. I was wondering if you had anything on Australia."

The silly expression on my face must have made his day.

Ruth greeted a gentleman similarly dressed with the usual apology that we had little in his field of interest in stock. He looked around the shelves anyway.

Since it was the appropriate time of year, early autumn and just after the High Holy Days, Ruth wished him a Happy New Year. It seemed a friendly thing to do. He swung round from the door, side locks flying.

"How do you know?"

She thought about it for a minute and then, as is traditional, she answered his question with a question.

"How do I know from your point of view or how do I know from my point of view?"

He had the grace to laugh.

On the whole, however, we learnt to keep any opinion about religion or politics to ourselves, subjects never to be discussed. The rules that guided the comportment of guests at the Victorian dinner table before port and cigars, held true for an Elizabethan book shop. But though the resolution is strong, the tongue sometimes slips.

The professor of history from a Canadian university seemed a smiling, friendly soul and keen to talk. He had a shock of hair, pleasantly creased face and untroubled, clear eyes. He wanted books about the Irish countryside. He was just on his way to Ireland. He was of Irish descent. In fact, he had just completed his magnum opus on the history of the religious divide in that country, the fruit of twenty years' work. I took the bait with no trouble at all. The best of my days during the previous years had been spent in a boozy corner of the Irish Republic and since I did not belong to either sect and could not even claim to be English, I took part in many a discussion in many a pub with careless freedom. It's an endless topic. A good friend once remarked that if you think you have the answer to the Irish problem, it's because you don't understand the question, but the amount of hot air spent trying was inexhaustible. To get a learned professor ready to talk about his subject with an unlearned bookseller was a rare pleasure, so I launched in, sweeping past the house rules without a qualm. The Canadian accent led me to assume that his stance would be as objective as mine.

He was charming, patient with my disbelief, supplied accurate references where I could only wave vaguely at allusions and allowed his unswerving fanaticism to seep into my consciousness gently. He had, in his days of innocence, held many of the opinions that I held still, but since then he had travelled the road to Damascus, a narrow path that left no room for compromise or compassion. He had bought a few little guide books and now was settling down comfortably, relaxed in the chair next to the desk. Customers came and went with their purchases and he smiled at them cheerfully, never losing the thread of an interrupted sentence. He was happy to spend time showing me the error of my opinions and the fundamental lack of validity of any questions I asked. I knew every weapon in his armoury ...

"Surely a woman as intelligent as you must see ..."

"The methodology we use today ..."

"It must be apparent ..."

"Even taking that into account, which I gladly do ..."

My arguments dried up. Fundamentalism can tolerate every strain, since it has filtered out all doubt. He left the shop at last, only to come back with a copy of the introduction to his book. As he turned in the door, he said a little prayer for my wellbeing.

I looked at the neatly bound typescript with some trepidation and wondered what I could say to him when he came to pick it up. What I read frightened me. It is rare to come across such erudite hatred, every barb resting in a well-honed sentence and every sentence laden with neatly balanced subordinated clauses and every clause coated in venom. The only consolation, I supposed, was that the book, once published, would only be bought by fanatics of the same colour. It was too dense and dull to incite riot.

On his return from Ireland, the professor, flushed with pleasure, came to collect his introduction. I asked if he had enjoyed his trip. He had. He had seen to the final details of the publication of his book and it would be ready in a matter of months. I reached for his folder wedged behind the desk.

"Thank you for allowing me to look at this," I simpered with unaccustomed sweetness.

"I'm sure it's very good but it really is too difficult for me, I'm afraid. I couldn't really finish it. But I did try. I just don't think that I really understand it."

He looked kindly at my crestfallen, humble face. Even fanaticism falters when faced with stupidity.

Ruth's fanatic was smoother and more sophisticated. Beautifully dressed, elderly, upright, soft-spoken, he had put together a small pile of expensive books and had accepted with courteous understanding her request that the cheque be cleared before he took the books away. He was a new customer and it was a simple precaution we took with large amounts. He praised our wisdom.

Whilst he had been selecting his books, another customer, a Mittel European, had been talking about some aspects of the history of the Austro-Hungarian Empire. Ruth had said very little since this particular man needed no encouragement and found other peoples' views distracting. His own, nevertheless, were very entertaining. The new customer, his transaction completed, now chose to enter the discussion. In almost accentless English he declared himself to be an Austrian and thus qualified to speak. With a hop and a jump he guided the discussion to the influence of the Jews and the corruption that they had brought to Austria. In the end event the court itself had not been immune. It was the turn of the old customer to be silent. Every aspect of Jewish contribution was pernicious and had infected Vienna with the degeneracy for which the only cure, in the end, had been Hitler. Would the Austrians otherwise have welcomed that runt? Yes, his family had been dispossessed by the Nazis but the National Socialists had been no more than an ill-conceived cure for a terminal disease. As to the so-called Golden Age at the turn of the century, that proved only how a parasite community could feed on the lifeblood of its host and then boast of the flower that it produced. He spat out a list of names that, to some, might indeed have represented the flower of art and learning, a cause for pride and respect. He had obviously delivered this speech before and he brooked no interruption though he spoke with calm. "Scum", "swine", "cancer" - he peppered his argument with invective without anger or passion, as if such words were normal when quietly telling a story or two to complete strangers in a bookshop.

He glanced at his watch and left the shop abruptly. Ruth put his cheque carefully into a drawer and looked at our old customer who stood looking at the door in unaccustomed silence.

After five full working days had passed, the tall Austrian came to collect his books. Slowly Ruth opened the drawer and took out his cheque.

"I have put the contaminated books back on the shelves." she said. She tore the cheque in two and handed him both halves.

"You would not wish to buy your books from scum."

After that I think we both tried to steer both our customers and ourselves from subjects that lit forest fires. Being merely human, it was difficult to remain entirely bland. There were many traps.

For instance, our shop was next to a shipping company. We were 9A and they were 9B. We had 9A clearly marked on our door and they had 9B on theirs. Yet their customers came puffing into our shop at regular intervals, tugging at cartons firmly knotted with rope, bulging cabin trunks, asking in round-eyed bewilderment in which obscure corner of this big city, 9B, New Cavendish Street might be found. Our neighbours were polite, gentle people so we often helped their customers through the thickets of New Cavendish Street, the 3.67 metres to their door, the elusive 9B. There was the occasion, however, when I was not feeling helpful and that was the day when a young man with a small parcel came in and very politely asked if by any happy chance I knew the location of 9B.

"Guess!" I invited.

"I don't know!" he said indignantly.

"Well," said I, ever the didact, "what does it say on the door behind you?"

"9A," he replied.

"And which letter of the alphabet comes after A?" I prodded gently.

"B," he said without a moment's hesitation.

Ready for the quantum leap, I asked, "So where do you suppose 9B will be?"

"I don't know," he said crossly, "I'm from Syria."

Without another word I led him next door. Inductive teaching can lead to forest fires.

However much wisdom we acquired over the years, it was never quite enough.

A small woman came into the shop, nodded vaguely in my direction with a faint smile and set to examining the books, title by title, shelf by shelf. Some she examined more closely and then slid back on the shelf. Some she handed to me with the same faint smile. The pile on my desk grew. After about two hours she glanced at her watch.

"I haven't finished," she said in a soft American accent, "but I have no more time today."

She took a card from her briefcase.

"I wonder if you would be good enough to invoice me and have the books shipped."

"Head of Collections, Las Vegas Public Library". I read and giggled.

"Las Vegas! I never imagined that you had a library there, of all places!" I blurted out.

She looked at me with some contempt.

"Certainly," she snapped. "We also have several schools and a hospital."

She left without another word.

The wisdom of Glendale sat on the door jamb with owlish wings folded and hissed at me.

Yet on another occasion, noted in the Day Book as a triumph of restraint, two gentlemen came in asking for 9B, dragging their baggage behind them. They were politely directed next door.

"Oh, do you have any Pope essays?" one of them asked in heavily accented English.

"By Pope or about Pope?" Ruth asked. He looked at her, unable to believe that anybody could be so dense.

"No!" he yelled.

Ruth immediately put her hand on the canister of tear gas we kept a few inches from our right hand. It was illegal. It was reassuring to know it was there, and though we never used it, there was more than one occasion when we drew without actually firing.

"No! No! Essays. I want Pope essays. That's like short stories without any point."

Ruth replied with scrupulous politeness that we were right out of pointless stories. He left. She put the tear gas back in its niche and awarded herself three Merit Stars in the Day Book, for distinguished conduct.

"How do you know the books are old? Some of them have no dates."
"Experience."

The wisdom lies in the brevity of the reply without any comment on the quality of the question. But that degree of restraint took years of yoga, martial arts and other schools of self-discipline.

The Bookdealer was a small, neat booklet that appeared weekly, which allowed us column space to list books we were looking for. The editors provided us with printed slips which we could fill out and send back when we found that we had in stock a book some other bookseller, somewhere else in England, was hoping to find for a customer. It wasn't a highly profitable part of the business but looking for wanted books was a service many of us offered and this was a fairly efficient way of finding books out of print or published abroad or just simply difficult to find. The Bookdealer had a wide circulation. On many occasions we were offered several copies of a book we didn't think we would find in a month of Sundays. There was a lot of pleasure to be had in phoning customers to tell them that we had found the book on fishing their grandfather had given them when they were ten, in the identical red binding, or the book of fairy tales they had first read on holiday on the Isle of Wight. There were books wanted by postgraduate students or grandmothers who wanted the books they had read as children to give to their own grandchildren, and they didn't want the modern reprints. Black Beauty was a popular title. The Railway Children was another. We tried to help where we could.

We explained plainly and carefully that we did not charge for this service. When we had a book we could offer them, should the search be successful, we would write or phone to see if the price met with their approval. Did they want a cheaper reading copy or a more expensive first edition in good condition? It wasn't very complicated. One customer wanted anything and everything we could find by Maurice Druon. When the week's slips arrived from the Bookdealer we found that we had been offered some thirty books and the range of titles was wide. Ruth put them aside, clipped in order of publication, for me to deal with, since I had been the one to offer this particular search. Well pleased with the stack of slips in front of me, I rang the customer to tell her the good news. I began to read the list of titles with our asking price; we added a small commission to the price asked by the bookseller in Southampton or Birmingham. In the case of Maurice Druon, the sums involved were very modest.

She stopped me.

"What do you mean?" she asked.

"I'm sorry," I said, "Was that more than you expected to pay?"

"But you didn't tell me I would have to pay anything when you offered to find the books for me," she shouted. "You never said anything about having to pay for them. You said quite distinctly that the service was free. People like you are quite disgraceful."

She slammed down the receiver and I sat in front of my thirty slips feeling evil. Our modest commission took on the weight of the worst kind of extortion. Could I really have explained it so badly that this degree of misunderstanding was possible?

I sought absolution in the day book but Ruth wasn't particularly sympathetic.

"Try shorter words and shorter sentences next time." she suggested.

Our shop was round the corner from the National Heart Hospital. We saw many patients taking their first walk round the block after open-heart surgery. For many we were a half-way staging post; our door was invariably open in the summer and we had a chair.

Roy was one of the patients who came into the shop on his first walk round the block. He was supported by his wife. His shock of white hair was the same colour as his face except that his skin had a primary coat of green. He shuffled, as if afraid the ground would fall away under his feet.

"Bypass," he muttered, as if explanation were needed. "Quadruple."

We offered him a glass of water. His wife drank it. We brought up another chair for her.

Roy was an illustrator and wanted to look at illustrated books. I turned the pages of W. Heath Robinson and Harry Clarke for him and he turned slightly rosy with pleasure. Over the next two weeks we saw him shed both the years and the pain. Soon he was in track suit and trainers gently jogging his mile round the block, stopping to wave but no longer stopping to rest. He was well enough to come to the shop with his wife as companion and not as crutch, and manage the weight of the books by himself.

Ruth and I agreed, wryly, that heart surgery would have to be added to the list of reasons for not buying a book. At the end of his stay, however, it was his wife and daughters who came in to buy books to celebrate his recovery and then his birthday. When he left hospital, the family moved to the country and he came in to see us every time he came for a check-up. We gained a valued customer. We also gained a health adviser. We learnt about pericarditis, angina pectoris, cholesterol levels, mitral stenosis, diet, exercise and more. With all the enthusiasm of the converted sinner, he was determined to drag us into the fold of the healthy.

I spend a good few months of my year in Chile, in the country, about an hour south of Santiago. It is not a country rich in antiquarian books but even in retirement the urge to look is strong. One of our many pleasures (my husband and I, not Ruth and I) is to wander round the flea market on Sunday morning, a flea market where a lot of goods for sale are laid out on the pavement and where an old radio with two knobs missing sits comfortably next to a set of rusty wrenches. There are books displayed, on shelves, in boxes. I still search for hidden treasure but after ten years I have found nothing more exciting than a tatty copy of Midshipman Easy and a mint first edition of an early novel by Harold Robbins.

On Saturday we often go to Patronato, a district where small shops are packed with handbags bearing too many chains and gilt trimmings, clothes with too many buttons, bows and sequins and underwear that should know better. Here we have lunch in a Korean restaurant where ours are the only two European faces. The streets are crowded and noisy.

"You go where?" say some of our Chilean friends. "I wouldn't go there to save my life. Franklin? Bio-bio! I've never set foot there."

Well, we have. Neither district is dangerous, just crowded and perhaps a little smelly.

Barrett Street was not in the least dangerous and rarely crowded. The plumbing, it is true, did sometimes let us down.

"Yes, that's exactly what I am looking for," said the voice on the phone. "but I am afraid that I simply do not go to those sort of places."

The voice was prissy, the vowels clipped. Ruth looked around at her surroundings, modest enough to be sure, but hardly meriting being described as one of "those sort of places".

"What sort of places?" she asked.

"Market. I don't go to markets."

"This is an Antique Market." she tried to explain. "It's not like a vegetable market."

"I am perfectly aware of that," he said briskly, "but it simply will not do. I wouldn't set foot there."

So an alternative arrangement was made.

She agreed to meet him outside the American embassy on Saturday at noon, bearing the desired Folio. He was to wear a red carnation.

My comment in the Day Book: "Sounds like John le Carré with additional dialogue by Groucho Marx. Don't forget the extra print. Have fun and don't lose anything you can't replace."

Her comment: "Do not worry, if I have to lose everything else, I shall hang onto the Folio."

And he wasn't our only dainty customer. There was a man who collected books illustrated by W. Heath Robinson and he did set foot in Barrett Street Market but decided that once was quite enough. Thereafter he rang regularly and invited Ruth to bring any book she had to offer to Fortnum and Mason where he, in turn, offered her a splendid tea with scones and clotted cream and miniature chocolate éclairs. He almost always bought the books she brought, wrote out a cheque straight away and helped her on with her coat. I was never invited.

Once we moved to Gray's the problem, such as it was, disappeared. We were in an Antique Gallery, on the Mayfair side of Oxford Street and thus totally respectable.

Tall, blonde and from Tulse Hill, she spent a long time looking at the old, illustrated book on dental instruments, an early rarety.

"Have you got a book you could let me see on corn-on-the-cob holders?"

Our non-sales were often totally respectable too. Sometimes they were honorable.

An old friend from way back when came into the shop and after happy hugs and exclamations were done, Ruth was invited to dinner. Although they had not seen each other for many years for all sorts of reasons, Ruth remembered Rosalind as a laughing iconoclast. In those days she had always been on the lookout for icons to tip over. She had waltzed down the aisle in a deep red wedding dress. In her first home she had a bedroom with a big bed and a dining room with a big table and dispensed with what was commonly called a Living Room, because, she said, she would not know what exactly one was supposed to live in one of those. She was an excellent cook, which took care of the big table; the rest was left unsaid.

So Ruth set off to dinner with a certain expectation of the unexpected. She was welcomed into a Drawing Room with two identical sofas facing each other across a large mahogany coffee table piled high with unopened books. There was a brass standard lamp, twin table lamps on twin tables with matching shades, softening the pools of light, as recommended by the best magazines. The colours all around were old rose and magnolia, picked out here and there with turquoise. Her fellow guests fell into the category of Accountant and wife, Bank Manager and wife and Solicitor and wife. The concession to "with it" informality was that the men wore their designer shirts without a tie and with the top button undone. The women, as if they had made a joint decision before opening their wardrobes, wore linen trousers and loose silk shirts with the labels sewn on the outside, considered more acceptable than leaving the price ticket dangling. Ruth did not have time to consider what to do with the first course, glaring at her in a glass bowl on a bed of crushed ice. That Rosalind should be serving something as banal as Prawn Cocktail was bad enough, but sea food brought Ruth out in big itchy weals and how do you announce that problem with accountant, lawyer and bank manager spooning theirs in with gusto? Then, there was the conversation to deal with. Who had seen the new play at the National? Who had seen the new film at the Odeon? Who had tried the new restaurant in Kensington High Street? Fine if you liked Japanese food. Who had read the new book by Doris Lessing or was it A. N. Wilson?

When the Accountant to her left asked Ruth how she filled her day, Ruth answered seriously and truthfully.

"How absolutely fascinating," said he, looking absolutely fascinated. "And where do you sell your books?" he asked with the indulgent smile of one expecting Ruth to keep her stock in a silken reticule.

"We have a shop between Marylebone High Street and Harley Street."

An address in London W1 could not be dismissed entirely as a ladies' playroom.

"Really?"

"Really."

"How delightful." said the Lawyer's lady.

"Not always." replied Ruth quietly.

"And what sort of books are they?" asked the Bank Manager.

"Old."

"Second-hand?"

"In the basement, yes. On the main floor they would be better described as antiquarian."

"Antiquarian! I say!" said the Accountant. "I suppose that's your euphemism for expensive."

"Yes." said Ruth without elaborating further.

"And do you specialise in anything in particular?" he asked, leaning forward with intelligent interest.

"Erotica and children's books." said Ruth, without elaborating further.

There was a slight clatter of spoons and Ruth found herself the happy centre of attention.

"Isn't that another of your euphemisms?" asked the Lawyer. "It's expensive pornography."

Ruth looked at him blankly, as if she was hearing the word for the first time in her life.

"Pornography?" she repeated, her French accent a little heavy on the vowels.

"Yes, pornography." he insisted.

"Well," she laughed, "we don't keep it on the top shelf."

"Where it belongs." said the Lawyer's lady.

"If it's by Goya or Picasso between hard covers with a three-figure price marked on the front end paper, you're allowed to keep it where you like."

Ruth was beginning to enjoy herself. She decided to enlighten the company, and the slight moue of disapproval all round kept her enthusiasm flowing.

"Of course, the French drawings in the eighteenth century are much more joyous than the German. They go in rather too much for whips and domestic animals. And the draftsmanship tends to be poor. No, German erotica simply did not attract the best, not until well into the nineteenth century." She wished she knew what she was talking about but no matter, she was having fun, so with the gravitas of an Oxford don drawing comparisons between Wittgenstein and Plato, she sailed on.

"The Dutch, of course, have always tended to go in for exaggerated private parts which never really caught on anywhere else. Their interest has never gone further than somewhat simplistic fornication, usually drawn in profile. Now the Russians are much more interesting but the material is difficult to come by, unfortunately, and they do tend to use inks that run, which can spoil the detail. The Oriental take on erotica is quite different from ours and the masterpieces that came out of the Floating World must be along the most collectable. The women curl their toes with pleasure ... but all in all, I prefer the French folios. The paper is beautiful and the binding often superb and you get the feeling that the husband may come in any minute and ruin the delicious moment ... yes, other than the Japanese, they have the greatest sense of style."

Eventually, with a little nod to the company, she finished her discourse and plunged into the chocolate mousse, a particular favourite that gave her no skin trouble at all.

On the Monday morning the Accountant came to call. She greeted him politely. He looked around casually.

The Solicitor came mid-week. Ruth asked after his wife and asked him to send her regards. He remarked on the quantity of children's books in stock. She agreed.

On Friday, when she had finally shut the door after the Bank Manager's visit, Ruth wrote in the day book:

"We're in the right business, just the wrong branch."

"Ship's rigging?"
"No, I'm sorry."
"Grief, why not?"
And the belligerent head withdrew from the door.

Ours was not a very big bookshop and we never pretended to cover all the philosophy between heaven and earth. We never failed to be amazed at the diversity of interests around us. There was, for instance, a small stack of books downstairs coyly marked "Romance", the result of one of those dumping expeditions by a young woman in a badly parked car. She had not even bothered to come back to see if we would pay her. The stack nourished some of the old ladies of Marylebone as well as one bald accountant in a striped suit. He bought two books at a time and every time he came to pay for them declared, in exactly the same words:

"For the wife, you know. In hospital."

After two years we became quite concerned for the poor lady's health.

Our favourite customers without any doubt were collectors completely steeped in their interest. They came in regularly, bright-eyed with hope and politely hiding their disappointment when yet again we had failed to find that rare jewel to crown their collection. They assumed that we knew as much as they did about their subject.

Under these circumstances it was always best to admit that we did not know the colour of Ian Fleming's eyes and without our reference book we could not disentangle the intricate fandango of rabbits and squirrels on the endpapers of the Beatrix Potter books but they were delighted to tell us. Men of age and stature sat pondering on the position of Squirrel Nutkin in the top righthand corner of the edition with buff boards. Women of Dresden delicacy searched for Blofeld in mint dustwrappers. There was a lady from the former East Germany, who must certainly have trained for the national discus or shot-putting team, who knew all there was to know about Victorian scraps and albums d'amitié. She handled pages of rose-infested putti and could tell us at which end of Nuremberg High Street they were printed.

A mysterious customer who came in regularly but never found anything exactly to her liking was a square, plain woman invariably dressed in anthracite worsted. She collected "oddball" material. It even said so on her visiting card. We offered a miniature globe. We offered a hand-made panorama carefully drawn and coloured by a child, signed and dated 1862. We offered hand-coloured board games, a small leather-bound volume called Le Cocu, not a commonplace subject for a book, however small, yet nothing we suggested was oddball enough. She was reticent about her collection. We asked if we might see what she already had, the better to understand what we needed to find. This was refused. We asked if "oddball" was an American or South African or Australian double speak for erotica but none of our colleagues had heard the expression used in that context. One of them, however, recognised the good lady from my description.

"The oddball woman? She stops by regularly. Last week she bought an alphabet."

"What was odd about it?" I asked.

"I have no idea. We're still trying to work it out."

Go know, as they say in some corners of the world.

The very elegant black woman came into the shop, looked around for a while and then turned to Ruth.

"What do you have on niggers?"

She enjoyed the appalled look on Ruth's face, there was no doubt. She paused a great deal longer than was necessary before she explained in her soft Southern drawl:

"I collect nigger material, mostly aimed at children, though not all of it. Golliwoggs. Wise niggers of the Uncle Tom school. Fat Mamas smiling benignly in plantation kitchens. Black and white ministrels."

"Have you found a lot in England?" Ruth asked. "Besides the 'Golliwogg books', that is."

This was a series of large oblong books, beautifully drawn stories recounting the adventures of a golliwogg doll, perfectly innocuous if you could accept the original premise.

"More than you'd imagine, given that you only traded in slaves but didn't sully home territory with them."

This was veering towards a Glendale no-go area. Ruth smiled blandly and showed her what we had. She bought everything.

"Do you have a list of what you already have in your collection? It will save a lot of time and correspondence," she asked.

Details were exchanged, hands shaken and the lady left in good humour.

Ruth wrote in the Day Book in letters bold.

"We need Nigger Material. Compose an advert for The Bookdealer that does not bring honorary membership of the BNP by return of post or a brick through our windows."

I tried. I produced a long-winded search request of irreproachable pomposity, which did bring some interesting offers and two anonymous phone calls, both venomous.

We met our fair share of straightforward enthusiasts, sailor, cook, needlewoman, photographer who assumed, so often, that our interest must be as great as theirs. Who, after all, can resist the finer points of ships' rigging? Unlike the book collector, however, they did not assume that our knowledge matched theirs. They always seemed to have the time and the patience to instruct.

We have little notes in the Day Books that mark their passage.

"I have learnt more to-day about the guts of a camera than I really need to know."

"The Medici were not good for Florence. If you have two hours to spare, I'll tell you why."

"If you are thinking about taking up fly fishing, as of to-day, I can make up the flies for you."

"The woman who collects shoes for lily feet came in with samples for our edification. I have cramp in my toes just from looking at them: Chinese torture in disguise. How horrible that they should be so beautiful."

"The Social History Man came in to-day."

This was a charming man completely absorbed in the minutiae of daily life in the seventeenth and eighteenth centuries in England. He knew about hooks and eyes, about needles, about the preparation of leather for making shoes, about the distribution of drinking water, about lords and beggars. He could and did talk about any given aspect of his beloved subject with passion. The one subject which appeared to have slipped past him was the manufacture of soap and personal hygiene. The gusts of body odour were acceptable in his chosen period; in a small shop in Marylebone two hundred years later, they were overwhelming. As he leaned over the desk to tell us about some fine point of interest he had spotted in a Newgate calendar, we wilted.

He came in one day in June. There was a great drop of rain hanging from the end of his nose. His hair was plastered to his head. He shook himself and glared furiously at the black clouds left safely outside the shop.

"Lord," he said, "this is awful. It's worse than having a bath!"

"Now how on earth would you know?" I did not say, I just opened the door wide and admired the cleansing downpour.

The ship's rigging enthusiast tried to persuade me that gut-wrenching seasickness was no obstacle to sailing.

"Look at Nelson!" was the inevitable example. It would have taken more than a column in Trafalgar Square to get me into a boat. I hoped that he would come on one of Ruth's days in the future. She loves sailing and has the grace not to talk to me about it.

We were told that anyone with a little application can weave their own version of the Bayeux Tapestry. A wooden palate is a mere detail if the desire to cook is there. All that is needed is the enthusiasm and a few really good books. Our two regular cookery enthusiasts were both very slim and I wondered sometimes if they talked their way through calories and enjoyed virtual sauces.

One of our young men was tracing Italian emigration through the adaptation of pizza recipes to the local ingredients. Apparently a pizza in Melbourne does not taste the same as a pizza in San Francisco and neither has the least resemblance to the Real Thing scooped out of an oven in Napoli. We helped him find books and articles which gave pizza even a passing glance. He told us a great deal about the quality of tomatoes here, there, then and now.

The enthusiast, as opposed to the obsessive collector, finds first editions and dustwrappers a decadent sophistication. Only the contents are important. They would not give the price of a bouillon cube for a signed copy, an association copy, the misplaced colon on page 53 of the first issue or the publisher's address missing from the second edition. Only the contents matter. So we listened enthralled as the beauties of the greater crested orchid or perhaps grebe were extolled and sank exhausted under the many uses of pomegranates in South Albanian cuisine.

Ruth fell under the spell of Alastair. His drawings are so seductive and subtle that Beardsley seems crude in comparison. There is a drawing of Manon being embraced in one of his illustrations for Manon Lescaut, and she has shed a slipper which is falling helter-skelter off the edge of the page.
"Have you ever seen anything more sensual than that shoe?" Ruth asked dreamily, holding the book out at arm's length. She had first option on any book by that artist that came our way and she put together a fine collection, including one original drawing. My unfettered enthusiasm was for Harry Clarke. There was a menace in his illustrations, even the most innocent, which appealed to me.

I rang the doorbell of his house in Dublin, now the property of The Irish Times, and trailed from attic to basement looking for his ghost. I sat in Bewley's, letting my tea get cold, gazing at his windows. I drove for miles on Irish roads looking for his stained glass in small unprized churches. I shook long hibernating curators who did not wish to have their dust unsettled. And I could talk about him for hours to anybody I could corner.
We were no worse than our best customers.

Chapter 8

The shop; The pleasures and tribulations

The first and immediate pleasure, throughout the years, was the sense of triumph. We hugged ourselves and each other as Glendale thrived.

We had worked our way from a small book room at home to a shop of our own. We had rent to pay, rates, electricity, telephone, insurance, bills that arrived with the precision of Greenwich mean time. We did our own cleaning. Rosemary worked for love of books and friendship more than for the pin money we paid her. The sons were expensive but we avoided their lipsmacking avarice most of the time.

We dropped "the shop" into our conversations to the point of boring friends and family but we failed to notice the glassy eyes and the yawns. We, naturally, were never bored and could and did discuss the position of every hinge and nail. We talked about our customers. We talked about our colleagues. We talked about sales. We talked about books. We talked.

The tribulations, in the early years, were not enormous. Our shopfront, for example, was designed by an architect who was so concerned with the uninterrupted line of beauty that he had not taken the comfort and delight of future occupants into account. Our plate glass door had no letter box. Our kind neighbours at 9B sheltered our orphan mail. Our door had a wide, gaping letter box at almost ground level, designed to keep the postman limber. There was a handsome gap at the top of our door. The howling winds that blew in had a chance to escape, however, through the equally handsome gap at the bottom of the door. Then slowly, almost imperceptibly, the door itself began to cause problems. It swung gently back to the closed position and stopped dead some six inches short of its destination. It needed a very hard shove to get it shut. Then, whatever lares and penates keep an eye on these things decided that they had not been properly propitiated and went into reverse, just to show us, so there. The door swung shut viciously, pushing and pulling unsuspecting customers off their feet.

"For heaven's sake, can't you do something about your door?" was one of the variations on a theme of irritation.

It would appear that an inaccessible spring should have been oiled regularly. Neglected and solid with rust, it cost the price of a decent time-share in Spain to get it replaced. We wondered if we should start a support group so that other victims of that architect and manufacturer of handsome doors could share our experience.

The hysterical behaviour of our door did bring into sharp focus how many people close the door behind them. If we had had a suitable stick, we would have made knotches. Did people close the door behind them at home? In winter to keep out the cold? In summer to keep out the flies? There was a fair amount of crabby speculation on the subject. Even-tempered Rosemary flipped from time to time as well.

I was moved to see if there was anything on the subject in our growing stock of etiquette books. These were a rare insight into social history and yet they were often bought for a laugh, which might explain a lot. These were the books I chose to check whenever we bought a new lot, and I could not resist reading a paragraph here, a chapter there. We listened to locals and tourists with all their varied accents, read passages to each other with whoops of laughter.

"Wait, just listen to this! Here's how to break off an engagement! Oh, and how to address a bishop and a duke. And you won't believe this! Punctuality! Four whole pages on punctuality."

Why should so many simple courtesies be no more than a joke? What is wrong with punctuality or closing a door gently behind you? I admit that the proper form of address for a duke or a nabob is not essential information for a workaday Monday morning, and the correct way to turn down the corner of your visiting card adds little to the wealth of nations, but does the pleasant have to be thrown out with the ornate affectation?

There have always been books for the spiritual and social guidance of the unruly tribes that came to form the major religious groups. Behaviour on earth was an integral part of one's prospects in the life (or lives) to come. They were etiquette books of the most honourable kind since they tried to deal with the manners of the heart and of the soul.

The etiquette books published after the Industrial Revolution had a different function. If the first generations of New Money were socially inept, the third and fourth generations had to be taught how to behave. The impoverished aristocracy could best plunder these riches through matrimony. The New Money was happy to save old family bacon if it meant a title for a daughter or an entrée to a ducal palace for a newly polished son. The middle classes, in all their various gradations, wanted to know how to get it right too. So began a whole industry. Chapters were written on the number of footmen needed, their livery, the size and shape of the cockade on a footman's hat (more than 5" was vulgar), the layout of a letter, comportment at times of mourning and detailed analysis of every courtesy. If the New Money was to be absorbed, society did not want to be disturbed. Those born neither to manor nor manner were expected to learn the customs of the class to which they aspired.

Later, there was a deliberate policy of encouraging a stricter morality and sense of responsibility to counter the rising crime rate in the 1860s. The books, with a whiff of fire and brimstone, which were written for this end, were not really etiquette books but since they often have chapters on how to behave, they slipped into that category on the shelves. Goodness, but they're grim.

The books on the education of children often leave nothing more than a sense of dread as well. I wish we could have cross-examined carefully the prospective purchasers of these litte handbooks. Were we, perhaps, teaching refined skills to child abusers? S. R. Hall, in his lectures to female teachers, recommends that children are qualified for happiness by being led to habits of submission.

Mrs Valentine suggests that young ladies should learn no more Latin than is needed to help a brother. Her thoughts on the French novel and the German and Italian languages in their entirety are not encouraging at all. The occupations suitable for a young lady's chaste hands, intricate, numbing and useless, are listed on three hundred tightly printed pages. Young women with an attitude, however wealthy, were not good marriage stock.

The text-books prepared for children are often frightening in their complete lack of imagination. Many are little more than lists of dry facts. The virtue of learning them well, out of gratitude to loving teachers and parents, is underlined at regular intervals. It's not surprising the Miss Bertrams went to the bad.

The fashion for etiquette books has not faded entirely. In the 1920s the emphasis changed. After the economic shifts following the Great War, what was needed was skill in keeping up appearances on a very diminished income and how to entertain without the services of a single servant (Have a dinner party on two successive evenings so that you can use the same flowers and make a trifle with other remains etc.). Those who were being taught to go up in the 1840s were now being taught to come down gracefully and to land on their uppers without a bump.

Today etiquette books deal with the knotty problems of sleeping arrangements for guests who are not married but do have a relationship. They discuss the vulgarities of coloured lavatory paper and the fine shades of upper- and lower-class language. At what time of the day you eat your dinner, if you sit on a sofa or a settee in your living room or your drawing room and if you use a toilet or a lavatory still seem to have some importance. Punctuality, the best way to end an engagement to cause the minimum distress, thank-you letters, their contents and lay-out, all get a mention. How to open or close a door when entering or leaving a bookshop had no relevance, whether before or after the Great War. I didn't even come across a footnote.

Perhaps it is the sudden, astonishing animus that inspires inanimate objects. We waited to see if the wretched door would start weeping tears or giving customers electric shocks by way of a star performance.

We had an old library trolley that we wheeled out every morning and wheeled in at night or when it rained. We filled it with temptingly inexpensive books. It must have caught its evil little spirit from the door. Every morning, we wedged all four wheels carefully. One morning, it kicked its wedges to one side and took off down the road. It hesitated only long enough to choose into which of the three parked cars it would crash. The deep blue, soft-top Rolls belonging to our neighbour (he made fancy curtains at fancier prices) was the obvious target and the trolley did not miss. The crash was heart-stopping. The trolley somersaulted in slow motion, the books fell neatly into the gutter, shelf by shelf, as our neighbour flew out of his shop, his unappetizing bouffant flapping round his bald patch. Can one reasonably apologise for the antic humour of a book trolley? Should one even be obliged to when our neighbour trod on our books to examine the bruises on his car's paintwork? Honour was frayed in New Cavendish Street.

After that, when I wheeled the trolley out in the morning, I talked to it gently but firmly. In the evening there was a word of praise if it had spotted a good Porsche at the parking meter and had resisted the temptation to take a run at it. Ruth just kicked the wedges in more firmly without a word. Again, her practical turn of mind; a trolley is a trolley and should be treated as such.

Later that year, I went home and left the thing out for the night. There's no excuse other than the absentmindedness which has been my downfall since schooldays. In the morning we found a note under the door to say that the trolley, together with its contents, had been taken into police custody (protective) and that we could collect our property at any time. A policeman on patrol had spotted it and had radioed for a van to come and take it away. It was very kind and our policemen are wonderful (book trolleys are not on drugs, are rarely black and never give you lip) but the only problem is that we did not own a van and nobody was prepared to wheel it home all the way from Portman Square. It's not a thing you can do nonchalantly. We organised help and I took a bunch of flowers to the police station as a token of thanks. I was told afterwards that though policemen may not accept gifts, my kind constable had been given dispensation from on high to take the flowers home. They had not been deemed to be in the blooms of corruption.

Ruth looked askance at me. She could not and would not see the funny side of it all. That practical turn of mind again.

"I cannot remember the last time I took any money."
Exaggeration was permitted in the day book.
"Comment annoncer au monde que nous sommes ici?"

"I am sitting all alone, in scarf, clutching hot soup like a road mender."
"The invasion was complete, your children, my children, friends for coffee and chat.
A customer? A client? A bibliophile? Whasat?"

"Could it be the knitting that's putting people off? L'odeur de vieilles et d'idiotie?"

The position of the shop, as we initially suspected and before wild optimism took over, was a disadvantage. The good residents of Marylebone did find us as did most of our old customers. It took time. We were tucked away just enough to be invisible if you were walking along the real New Cavendish Street with your head down. So when unusually quiet days happened, and they certainly happened those first two or three years, we saw ourselves rushing to the bottom of the Northern Line on our fancy business projection.

But then, there were the high days when the whoops and the triumph filled the day book without humility or restraint. BLOCK LETTERS in red were in order.

There was a queue at the desk to pay. Cheap reading copies, signed limited editions in their original boxes, and there was no pattern or rhyme or reason why that particular third Thursday of the month the shop flourished where the preceding Wednesday had drawn a complete blank.

"I could have done with an extra pair of hands today," scrawled Ruth. "Have we sold out?"

"There were three people waiting when I opened the door.
I've been run off my feet. It's a quarter to four."

"I've sold two limited Rackhams, cream vellum and gold,
Walter Crane and that Bible long lingering unsold."

"Battered paperback romance, Bakst, Vanity Fair,
Don't look for Sir Walter, he's no longer there,
Charles Perrault left this morning. Grimm went off after tea.
There's the desk left, a tired sandwich, the Day Book and me!"

On one of my very busy days, by four o'clock my sandwich too had curled and my orange juice was tepid, but still they came and I was tired.

So when in the afternoon, soon after five o'clock, Son No. 2 poked his head round the door, I was delighted.

"D'yer want a lift home?"

What can be more welcome on a Friday afternoon than such a gracious offer? The thought of a car outside the door was wonderful.

I decided that I would not put out the rubbish, reconcile the cash, finish the notes in the day book, tidy the desk or do any of those small Friday chores that make the shop pleasant for my partner on Monday morning. To hell with it!

I had the offer of a lift home and my feet were singing hallelujahs of relief. I wheeled in the trolley with the paperbacks, grabbed the paying-in book and in less than three minutes declared myself ready to go.

In the car my son was very quiet. As we joined the traffic jam in Marylebone Road he began to mutter.

"Funny."

"What's funny?"

"Nothing really."

"So why are you muttering? Look where you're going and concentrate."

"No. No. I'm sure you know what you're doing." he said at the next lights, shaking his head.

"Since when? And anyway, what are you talking about?"

"It's just that I didn't see you switch off the lights downstairs."

"Of course I did!"

This was like hinting to your average holidaymaker, just after take-off, that perhaps the gas had not been turned off. All certainty evaporates.

"And I'm not sure that I saw that young man come up. Do you know the one I mean? Bald patch and lime-green trousers."

My son, I suspected, was enjoying himself.

"Don't be ridiculous and turn the car round." I snapped.

And so it was, dear reader, that we found a captive customer, sitting reading comfortably, waiting for someone to remember him and open the door. He appeared quite unperturbed. The hysterics were all mine.

Other than a blocked lavatory, the worst that can happen in a bookshop is a dead telephone. October 1992 was our moment of major telephone tribulation.

The "Open Letter to British Telecom" was written in the hope that humour might help, either us or that distinguished public company.

AN OPEN LETTER TO BRITISH TELECOM

Sirs,

Quarto, Folio, calf, cloth, first or second impression, printed in Amsterdam or Ambleside, all pales into insignificance when the telephone is not working.

'Twas on a Monday morning when my partner picked up the receiver to find that the line was dead. The engineers were informed by our (long suffering) neighbours. On Monday afternoon the engineers had still not yet appeared. We were told indignantly when we phoned (neighbours still suffering) that the engineers had indeed called twice but the premises were empty. Oh? And where had they called? Ah, it would seem that the address on the records was incorrect. How strange that the telephone bills, bearing precisely the correct address, find their way to our door with such teutonic punctuality.

'Twas on a Tuesday morning that the engineers were sent twice more to the wrong address. By the early afternoon, having defied the gravity of BT records, they found us. They checked the lines in the shop but could go no further because the main junction box is sensibly located in the basement of the block of flats of which our shop forms part of the ground floor and access can only be had through the good offices of the caretaker. He hasn't had a good office since God was a Lieutenant. In fact he's a one-man obstacle course well known even to the telephone engineers.

'Twas on a Wednesday morning that the telephone engineers were graciously permitted to inspect the junction box. They found the fault and marked it for the outside engineer who came in the afternoon. He came in, went out, came in and went out again. He sucked his teeth and shook his head. At 2.30 p.m. he picked up the receiver and announced triumphantly that all was well. We had a dialling tone.

We did indeed. A dialling tone so solid that it could not be broken. At 2.45 p.m. we phoned the service manager's office once more (our neighbours are looking a little strained) but

'Twas not until Thursday morning the outside engineer came to call. Once more we moved books and shelves to let him test all the bits and pieces. He tapped and probed. He was not happy. He called in a second opinion. A new line was needed. It would be done with all speed and expedition but not until after lunch. And so, with the shop in chaos, two lines were put in and

'Twas on a Friday morning that M. & R. Glendale went back to work.

We wish to be recompensed for loss of profit, loss of nervous energy and the cost of a couple of very good bottles of wine for our neighbours.
Yours faithfully,
M. D. SEARS
with humble homage to Flanders & Swann.

The matter of the telephone was resolved. Such matters always are, though rarely to the entire satisfaction of the customer.

The Business Customer Service Manager had sent our plaint to an equally charming and efficient officer in Drury Lane. Where better? There was something theatrical about British Telecom's Customer Service.

After a month of silence I rang to find out how we were all getting on. She was busy and would ring me back. She didn't. I tried again. She was on leave for a week. I tried a week later and was put on to Miss Karla Mistry (sic).

"What can I do to help you, Monika?" she purred (The Girl with the Golden Phone; central casting has much to answer for).

She offered lean compensation.

"What is the position on loss of earnings?" I asked.

"We will do our best to help, Monika."

I gritted my teeth and continued to address her as Miss Mistry. Nothing makes me feel as belligerently of the Old School as the use of my first name by someone I haven't even seen. Suddenly I had one friend more than I had voted into my affections and she was bending rules and regulations just to help little bad-tempered me, to comfort me for the loss of my telephone for too many days. She cooed and she soothed and promised to send me the application form needed to claim loss of earnings, together with all the information I would need for triumph and success.

It all arrived in a beautiful folder the following morning, decorated with a jovial little logo, a drawing of a pen drawing the sunniest of smiles across the cover. Service was guaranteed. Confidence was high. All I had to do was to fill in the form, produce a set of accounts, a detailed statement from our accountants, our cash records with a clear statement of how the loss had been calculated, details of gross profit and an "after tax" figure. Eazy peazy. I rang Miss Mistry and told her that I would be delighted to accept the figure she had quoted in the first place. Our accountant has no idea how lightly he has got off.

The cheque, when it arrived, covered the cost of 1½ of the bottles of wine we had delivered to 9B, the people with a functioning telephone. And we hadn't been to Berry Bros., just the local Oddbins.

In 1993 the social life was fine but it was no use pretending that business was good. The valentines continued to sell well at the beginning of February. The kettle was in good working order and old friends had a usual amount of time to sit and sip coffee. The radio bulged with oratory, justification and sober predictions that the yellow-brick road offered by the party manifests was the only way to the elusive bright tomorrow when people bought expensive books. The only certainty was that politicians would win the next election.

Over the previous year or two, the shopscape in Marylebone High Street changed. Leases fell in and were not renewed at the new economic rents; this particular definition of economics simply meant multiplying the previous rent by three or four. There is a limit to the number of lamb chops a butcher can sell and a limit to how high he can hoist up the price he charges for them. A modest familiarity with basic arithmetic showed that turnover and overheads were not going to make economic sense by any definition, from the tenant's point of view. The butchers left, the bakers closed and the greengrocers faded away. A new supermarket opened and then another. Shops stayed empty and then were let on a temporary basis to charity organisations. Filled with the bric and the brac of cleared wardrobes and kitchen cupboards, the windows were dressed unappealingly by good-hearted volunteers with the best of the donations. A weary Dior, but a Dior for all that, hung limply on a chipped dummy with a three-cup/five-saucer tea service at its feet. They invariably had boxes of books on offer, travel and restaurant guides of yesteryear and a surfeit of souvenir issues celebrating royal marriages long since in pieces. One sad year we counted eleven such shops along the High Street as we walked to the underground station.

Two shops became branches of two more building societies as two charity shops withdrew, their window displays replaced by bright posters vaunting a further nonopercent interest on your investment. Then we were offered beautiful shoes with matching handbags at imaginative prices in the shop that had once sold bread. The three new dress shops vied with each other flounce for flounce. The sizes they stocked ranged from anorexic to skinny; size 12 was labelled "large". The hardware shop gave way to expensive lighting. More charity shops disappeared to make way for French furniture and household goods designed with fashionable Shaker simplicity, their astonishing price tickets handwritten on recycled paper. A shop selling new books specialising in travel opened its doors. Good books intelligently displayed, sold by people who know their stock made a welcome pause on the way to and from the station.

Was this progress? Were we turning up our noses at change because we were getting older and sentimental nostalgia was taking the place of common sense. Sensible people must prefer a good supermarket where everything can be bought under one roof out of the rain. It must be more convenient than traipsing from shop to shop up and down the high street, wasting time on greetings and chat.

At the end of ten years, Marylebone High Street had become another elegant boulevard and we glared at it, disconsolate.

Perhaps this cranky view of our little world was a way of cushioning the blow we both knew was on its way. The hard-working Turkish gentleman who sold hamburgers and resplendent jacket potatoes overflowing with cholesterol told us that his lease had just come up for renewal. The rent demanded, two and a half times what he was paying, left him speechless. Hamburgers and overloaded jacket potatoes were not going to stretch their way round that rise even if all his satisfied customers lived on nothing else for a month, so he, too, like the butcher and the baker, faded away.

The surveyor came, gave the place a perfunctory flick with one professional eye, added two runes to the many clinging to his clipboard and left. For us, the visit spelt Schedule of Dilapidations. We could no longer avoid the subject of The Lease, which was rapidly coming to an end. For months we had avoided the subject. Last year, when one tried to bring the conversation round to it, the other would say, very cheerfully, "Well, let's see what happens.".

The recession could not go on indefinitely. There was to be an election. Promises were being made. The CBI was indicating a measured upturn. We read the Financial Times and felt equipped to comment.

"Well, we shall see what happens." we recited sagely.

The months passed. The costs crept up. The turnover crept down. We waited. The letter came and advised us that our rent was to be muliplied by four, should we wish to renew our lease.

We could not afford the new rent, together with the Unified Business Rate, a close cousin of the unloved Poll Tax.

So the decision took itself. We could not afford to renew the lease and that was that. We understood that this was not a local crisis, had a small insight into the interweaving of industrial economics that have managed to get themselves knotted, the blight of over-production, loss of markets, the unbalances caused by removal of the war footing, Eastern European destabilisation, third-world debts and even the greenhouse effect. Our shop was but one tattered thread in life's exhausting tapestry. You cannot say to a people counting grains of rice "Let them eat antiquarian books!" No, on a global scale our shop was not a feature.

The trouble was that we found it difficult to live on a global scale. It was difficult to avoid the niggling thought that multiplying our rent and that of our many neighbours had a hint of opportunism about it. Our landlords, for all their impeccable turn of phrase and correctly punctuated letters on heavy bonded paper, were riding on the back of the greatest economic realignment since the Industrial Revolution. They were filling their coffers for no economic reason that any economist could explain. Their arrogance was hardly veiled by courtesy; the appointment we requested in order to discuss the matter was refused. There was nothing to discuss. No negotiation was possible.

We were fond of our shop and it was hard to give it up. We made all sorts of sensible, comforting noises at each other, all completely useless.

We would miss the stimulus, the unexpected questions, the treasures and the dog-eared paperbacks offered for our inspection. We would miss the spiritual exercise of smiling sweetly when deep inside we wanted to wring a neck.

We made sensible plans. We would organise a Book Room. But wasn't that where we came in? Yes, but now we were older, wiser, with some knowledge and experience. We would exhibit at more international fairs. Well-meaning friends pointed out how much more time we would have to travel, to discover the rare and the wonderful. But we knew that the rare and the wonderful were more likely to be hiding between the sturdy cloth covers of a book than in the life of a bookseller. Fiction was best treated as fiction.

Think of all we would save on overheads! We had dealt with our overheads efficiently. Overheads were part of running a business, however big, however small. We had not costed in two sports cars and an executive jet; the new rent demand was over our heads, and that was out of control.

So we made a decision, set a date, informed our landlords, inserted a note in The Bookseller and sat like two birds on a wire, not looking at each other. When her marriage broke up, I was there for her. When my son fell out of a window, she was there for me. We had managed to have the hard times of our lives in turn so that there was always one standing vertical with life-belt and lasso. Now we sat in our shop, whilst it was still ours, and stopped pretending that we were going to make the best of it. We were angry and miserable and defeated. Who can take pleasure in a Post Office Box, who has once had an antiquarian bookshop of their own?

During the last two weeks, business could not have been brisker. Some spirit with a malevolent sense of humour had wound up the clockwork and set us to the serious business of selling books. We did not renew the stock. We did not work in turn but came to the shop together. The pay-in book was taken to the bank with a pleasing bulge. Every post brought in orders and requests for a search.

It also brought a letter from our landlords asking if we wished to make an appointment with a view to renegotiating the terms of our lease. Our reaction is not fit to print in any of the several languages at our command.

We dealt with years of accumulated rubbish, the telephone directories long out of date, the boxes of elastic bands, files of newspaper articles, the fridge and the music stand.

Ruth and I looked at our lovely shop in dumb misery. A bookshop is not like any other shop. It grows a crust of good dust over the years and ours was just getting comfortable. Chaos need only be ordered round the edges. Books on obscure subjects attract the eccentric and the off-beat and both are welcome. Neglected paperwork adds to the comfort of the chaos. The stock has a limitless shelf life. The customers are rarely in a hurry and rarely rude. A bookshop is the best place to find rest for a troubled mind, whether as seller or as buyer. Now you can't give up all that without a whine.

We have moved on. Ruth is still involved with books, searching and accumulating for a library. I still get a pang when I see a small antiquarian bookshop in Paris or Bucharest or Montevideo. Fifteen years have passed and I think we are still whining but only to each other.